BCBA Test Prep

The Essential Guide to Passing the Board Certified Behavior Analyst (BCBA) Exam

Jennifer Meller

Contents

Chapter One

Introduction

Welcome to the beginning of your journey towards becoming a Board Certified Behavior Analyst (BCBA). This esteemed certification is awarded by the Behavior Analyst Certification Board (BACB), which signifies a standard of excellence in the principles and practices of Applied Behavior Analysis (ABA).

The BCBA exam is a rigorous assessment that evaluates your understanding and application of behavior analytic principles, ethical considerations, and strategic interventions. To achieve success, it's essential to grasp not only the theoretical underpinnings of the field but also how to apply this knowledge in practical, ethical, and effective ways.

In this introduction, we will outline the structure of the BCBA exam, the domains covered, and the types of questions you can expect. We'll also share strategies for preparation that align with the BACB's task list and ethical guidelines. Our goal is to equip you with a robust framework that prepares you not just for the exam, but for a rewarding career contributing to the well-being of individuals through the power of ABA.

As we proceed, we will delve into each domain of the BCBA task list, providing detailed explanations, real-world examples, and practice scenarios. By the end of this guide, you will have a comprehensive understanding of the exam's content and how to approach studying effectively.

Remember, the BCBA exam is not only a test of knowledge but also a reflection of your commitment to the highest standards of behavior analysis. Let's embark on this educational journey together, building the knowledge and skills that will underpin your future success as a BCBA.

***

Overview of the Book's Structure

This book is organized to provide a structured and comprehensive approach to preparing for the BCBA exam. It is divided into several key sections, each focusing on different aspects of the exam and the field of behavior analysis. Below is an overview of the book's structure:

1. **Introduction**: Sets the stage for your preparation journey, providing context and understanding of the BCBA exam's importance.

2. **Understanding the BCBA Exam**: A detailed look at the exam's format, question types, and scoring system, along with registration details and important dates.

3. **Foundational Knowledge**: Covers the basic principles and concepts of behavior analysis that form the foundation of the field.

4. **Principles of Behavior**: Explores the core tenets of behavior analysis, including reinforcement, punishment, stimulus control, and more.

5. **Assessment in Behavior Analysis**: Discusses the methods and importance of conducting behavioral assessments and collecting data.

6. **Behavior Change Procedures**: Offers insights into the various intervention strategies and their ethical considerations.

7. **Supervision and Management**: Focuses on the roles and responsibilities of BCBAs, including best practices for supervision.

8. **Ethics in Behavior Analysis**: A critical examination of the ethical standards governing the practice of behavior analysis.

9. **Exam Preparation Strategies**: Provides tips and techniques for studying, managing time, and dealing with test anxiety.

10. **Practice Questions and Answers**: Includes a collection of practice questions with in-depth answers to simulate the exam experience.

11. **Resources for Further Study**: Lists additional materials and resources for a more extensive review.

12. **Appendices**: Contains supplemental materials such as checklists, glossaries, and indexes.

Each section is designed to build upon the previous one, ensuring a layered understanding of the material. By working through this book, you will gain a deep comprehension of behavior analysis and be well-prepared to take and pass the BCBA exam.

***

Tips on How to Use This Guide Effectively

1. **Establish a Study Schedule**: Allocate specific times for study each day and stick to your schedule. Consistency is key to retaining information.

2. **Active Learning**: Engage with the material actively. Don't just read; take notes, highlight important concepts, and teach them to someone else.

3. **Use Practice Questions**: After studying a section, test your knowledge with practice questions. This will help you identify areas where you need more review.

4. **Form Study Groups**: If possible, join or form a study group. Discussing concepts with peers can enhance understanding and retention.

5. **Take Regular Breaks**: Study in intervals—typically 25 minutes followed by a 5-minute break. This method can improve focus and prevent burnout.

6. **Reach Out for Support**: If you're struggling with a concept, don't hesitate to seek help from a mentor, colleague, or online forum.

7. **Review Regularly**: Revisit previous chapters regularly to keep the information fresh in your mind.

8. **Stay Informed**: Keep up-to-date with any changes to the BCBA exam structure or task list by checking the BACB website.

By following these tips and utilizing this guide as a comprehensive resource, you can optimize your study time and approach the BCBA exam with confidence.

Chapter Two

Understanding the BCBA Exam

Structure and Format of the Exam

The BCBA exam is designed to assess your knowledge and skills necessary to function as a behavior analyst. It is a comprehensive test that encompasses a wide range of topics within Applied Behavior Analysis (ABA). Here's a breakdown of the structure and format:

- **Computer-Based Testing**: The exam is administered via computer at various testing centers worldwide.
- **Question Format**: The questions are primarily multiple-choice, each with four possible answers.
- **Number of Questions**: The exam typically consists of 160 questions, with a specified number being pretest (unscored) questions.
- **Duration**: You will have a set amount of time to complete the exam, often four hours.
- **Content Areas**: The exam covers specific content areas outlined in the BACB's task list, which reflects the current practice of behavior analysis.
- **Scoring**: The exam is scored using a scaled method, with a certain score required to pass.

Understanding the structure and format of the BCBA exam is crucial to effective preparation. With this knowledge, you can tailor your study approach to the specific demands of the test, focusing on time management, question format familiarity, and comprehensive coverage of the content areas.

***

Types of Questions Encountered

The BCBA exam primarily features multiple-choice questions that are designed to assess a wide range of competencies in applied behavior analysis. These questions may include, but are not limited to:

- **Scenario-Based Questions**: These questions provide a situation or case study and ask you to select the most appropriate action or interpretation based on ABA principles.
- **Definition and Concept Questions**: These require you to identify definitions or concepts that pertain to behavior analysis terms or principles.
- **Application Questions**: These questions assess your ability to apply ABA principles and techniques to hypothetical scenarios.
- **Data Interpretation Questions**: You might be given graphs, data tables, or research summaries and asked to interpret the information or suggest next steps based on the data.
- **Ethical Dilemmas**: These questions are designed to assess your understanding of the Professional and Ethical Compliance Code for Behavior Analysts.

As you prepare for the exam, it is important to become comfortable with these types of questions and to practice applying your theoretical knowledge to these practical query formats.

***

Grading Criteria and Passing Scores

The BCBA exam uses a scaled scoring system. This means that the raw scores (the number of questions answered correctly) are converted to a scaled score that considers the difficulty of the questions. The scaled score needed to pass the BCBA exam is determined by the Behavior Analyst Certification Board (BACB) and is subject to change. It's essential to check the BACB's official resources for the most current passing criteria. Generally, a scaled score represents your performance relative to the established standards, rather than a percentage correct. It's designed to ensure consistency in the level of proficiency required to pass, regardless of which version of the exam is taken.

***

Registration Process and Exam Dates

To register for the BCBA exam, candidates must first apply through the Behavior Analyst Certification Board (BACB) and provide evidence of having met all eligibility requirements. Once the application is approved, candidates will receive instructions on how to schedule their exam. The exam is offered continuously throughout the year, allowing candidates to choose a date and time that is most convenient for them at one of the many Pearson VUE testing centers worldwide.

For specific dates, registration deadlines, and detailed instructions on the application process, it's important to refer to the official BACB website or contact the BACB directly, as this information can change periodically.

Chapter Three

Foundational Knowledge

Foundational knowledge in behavior analysis covers a range of concepts that form the basis of understanding behavior from a scientific perspective. Some of the basic concepts in behavior analysis include:

Operant Conditioning: Think of this as the heart of behavior analysis. It's like a conversation between actions and consequences. When you do something that's followed by a 'high-five' from life (a positive outcome), you feel good and are likely to do it again, right? That's positive reinforcement. Conversely, if life gives you a 'time-out' (a negative outcome), you might think twice before doing that action again.

Reinforcement: It's your personal cheerleader for behaviors! Positive reinforcement is like getting a gold star sticker for a job well done, making you want to do it again. Negative reinforcement is like the relief you feel when a headache goes away after taking medicine, encouraging you to use that remedy again in the future.

Punishment: If reinforcement is the carrot, punishment is the stick. It's there to gently nudge behaviors to appear less frequently. Positive punishment might be adding extra chores when rules are broken, while negative punishment could be losing access to your favorite video game for a while.

Discriminative Stimulus (SD): These are the signals in our environment that tell us it's a good time for certain behaviors. It's like a green light signaling when it's okay to cross the street of behavior.

Functional Assessment: This is like being a behavior detective. You're looking for clues to understand why a behavior happens. Is it for attention, a break from work, or maybe access to toys? Figuring this out helps us address behaviors more effectively.

Generalization and Discrimination: Generalization is the ability to apply what you've learned to new, similar situations. It's like using your knowledge of baking cookies to try making a cake. Discrimination, on the other hand, is knowing when certain rules apply and when they don't, like understanding that you can't bake a cake the same way you microwave popcorn.

Shaping: This is about celebrating the small steps on the way to a big goal. It's like cheering for every milestone during a marathon, not just the finish line. Each little success is a step in the right direction.

Extinction: Imagine a vending machine that stops giving snacks when you insert money. If this keeps happening, you'll stop using it, right? That's extinction — when a behavior no longer gets the result you want, you're less likely to do it.

Behavioral Chains: These are sequences of actions that link together to form a routine. Each step triggers the next, like a dance routine where each move is a cue for the next step.

As you cozy up with these concepts, picture them in action in your daily life. This isn't just textbook material; it's the real, vibrant science of behavior that you'll use to make meaningful changes in the world. Keep these principles close to your heart as you continue on your journey to becoming a BCBA. They are the tools that will empower you to understand and shape behavior in profound ways.

***

Definitions and Terminology

In behavior analysis, definitions and terminology are the building blocks that help us communicate complex concepts clearly and precisely. Here's a cozy overview to make these terms feel more like familiar friends than abstract ideas:

- **Behavior**: Simply put, it's an action or a response that can be observed and measured. It's what we do, and it's at the center of what behavior analysts study.

- **Stimulus**: Think of it as anything that can influence behavior. It's like a nudge or a whisper that can prompt an action or a response.
- **Reinforcer**: This is a special kind of stimulus that follows a behavior and makes that behavior more likely to happen again. It's like the secret sauce that adds flavor to our actions, making us want to serve them up more often.
- **Contingency**: This term captures the idea of a 'if-then' relationship between behavior and its consequence. It's the rulebook that says if you do this, then that will happen.
- **Consequence**: It's the result or outcome that follows a behavior. Just like cause and effect, it tells us what happens after an action is taken.
- **Rate**: This is all about how often a behavior happens. Think of it as the rhythm of actions over time.
- **Duration**: This measures how long a behavior lasts. It's the stopwatch that keeps track of how much time a behavior takes up.
- **Latency**: It's the time delay between a cue and the start of a behavior. It's like the pause before you start singing after hearing the first note of your favorite song.
- **Magnitude**: This refers to the intensity or force of a behavior. It's the volume knob for actions.

Each term is a thread in the tapestry of behavior analysis. As you get to know them, you'll be able to weave them together to understand and shape behavior in meaningful ways. Remember, these aren't just words; they're tools to unlock the mysteries of why we do what we do.

***

Historical Perspectives and Key Figures

The field of behavior analysis is deeply rooted in the early 20th century when psychology was evolving to more scientifically rigorous methods. John B. Watson championed behaviorism, insisting psychology should be observable and measurable. He conducted famous experiments, like the Little Albert study, emphasizing environmental impact on behavior.

Then came B.F. Skinner, a towering figure who expanded upon behaviorism to develop operant conditioning. He introduced concepts like reinforcement and punishment, showing that behavior could be shaped by consequences. His novel experiments and theories, detailed in works like "The Behavior of Organisms," provided a pragmatic approach to behavior modification.

Ivan Pavlov's work on classical conditioning revealed how associative learning occurs, which is foundational to understanding how involuntary responses can be conditioned by stimuli. His legacy is the famous 'Pavlov's dogs' experiment.

Albert Bandura introduced social learning theory, demonstrating the power of observation and imitation in learning. His 'Bobo doll' experiments highlighted how individuals learn from the environment, not just through direct experience but also by observing others.

These key figures laid the intellectual groundwork for contemporary behavior analysis, influencing how therapists, educators, and even parents understand and guide behavior. Their collective contributions have paved the way for a scientifically supported approach to behavior modification, which now underpins the practices you will learn as a BCBA.

Chapter Four

Principles of Behavior

When we delve into Chapter 3, "Principles of Behavior," we focus on two fundamental concepts that are at the heart of behavior analysis: reinforcement and punishment. These principles help us understand how behaviors are acquired, maintained, or modified. Let's explore each concept with a touch of warmth and clarity to ensure a deeper understanding.

Reinforcement is like the warm sunlight for a plant; it helps behaviors to grow and flourish. When a behavior is followed by a favorable outcome, that behavior is more likely to be repeated in the future. Reinforcement can be positive, where something desirable is added (like praise or treats after a job well done), or negative, where something unpleasant is removed (like the relief one feels when a headache fades away after taking medicine). Both types of reinforcement increase the likelihood that the behavior they follow will be repeated.

Punishment, on the other hand, can be thought of as a bitter wind that discourages plants from growing in certain directions. It's a consequence that decreases the likelihood of a behavior occurring again. Just like reinforcement, punishment can be positive or negative. Positive punishment involves adding something unpleasant after a behavior (like scolding), while negative punishment involves taking away something desirable (like removing a child's toy following undesired behavior). Despite their names, 'positive' and 'negative' don't mean 'good' or 'bad'; they simply indicate whether something is being added or removed.

Understanding these principles isn't just academic; they are tools that can shape behavior in practical, compassionate, and effective ways. By applying these concepts thoughtfully, you can encourage behaviors that enhance learning, growth, and well-being.

Here are real-life examples of reinforcement and punishment:

Reinforcement:

- **Positive Reinforcement:** A parent gives their child a sticker each time they put away their toys. The child likes receiving stickers, so they start putting away their toys more often.
- **Negative Reinforcement:** An office worker has a headache and takes an aspirin. The aspirin removes the headache, so the next time they have a headache, they are likely to take an aspirin again.

Punishment:

- **Positive Punishment:** A teenager stays out past curfew and, as a result, their parents reprimand them. If the teenager wants to avoid being scolded, they might come home on time in the future.
- **Negative Punishment:** An employee is consistently late, so the manager decides to revoke their privilege of flexible work hours. The loss of this privilege may motivate the employee to start arriving on time.

Each of these scenarios showcases how behaviors can be influenced by the consequences that follow them, which can be especially useful in shaping behavior in educational settings, parenting, workplace management, and personal development.

***

Stimulus Control

Stimulus control is a term used in behavior analysis to describe situations in which a behavior is triggered by the presence or absence of some stimulus. Here are some real-life examples of stimulus control:

1. **Traffic Lights and Pedestrian Crosswalks:**
   - Beyond simply telling drivers when to go or stop, traffic lights also control pedestrian behavior. When the walk signal appears, it signals pedestrians that it's safe to cross the street. Conversely, when the don't-walk signal or a flashing hand appears, it signals them to wait. This is a learned behavior based on the consequences of safety when following the signals and potential danger when not.
2. **Classroom Settings:**
   - In a classroom, the teacher's presence at the front of the room often serves as a stimulus for students to pay attention and be quiet. The teacher may use a specific signal, like raising a hand or ringing a bell, to gain students' attention or indicate that the class should start. These specific stimuli control the students' behavior, leading them to focus on the teacher rather than engaging with classmates or other distractions.
3. **Work Environments:**
   - In many workplaces, the stimulus might be the sound of a whistle or buzzer indicating the beginning or end of a break. Workers learn to associate these sounds with ceasing or starting work-related tasks. The consistent pairing of the stimulus (the sound) and the consequence (the work activity or rest period) establishes a strong stimulus control over behavior.
4. **Daily Routines:**
   - The presence of specific environmental cues can signal behaviors associated with different times of day. For instance, the setting of the sun can trigger a routine of locking doors, dimming lights, and preparing for bed. Conversely, sunrise may serve as a stimulus for starting the day, opening blinds, and beginning morning routines.

5. **Animal Training:**

    - Trainers often use stimulus control to teach animals behaviors. A trainer might use a whistle as a stimulus to signal a dolphin to jump or a dog to sit. The animals learn that the presence of the whistle sound means a reward is available if they perform the correct behavior. Over time, the behavior becomes controlled by the stimulus of the whistle.

6. **Marketing and Consumer Behavior:**

    - Stimulus control is also evident in consumer behavior. For instance, sales signs in store windows are stimuli that can influence the behavior of customers, prompting them to enter the store and make purchases. Similarly, the smell of food from a bakery can trigger hunger and attract customers.

In each of these examples, behavior is under the control of specific stimuli because the behavior has been reinforced in the presence of those stimuli in the past. This relationship is built through experience and learning. The consequences of the behavior (whether reinforcement or punishment) ensure that the behavior is likely to be repeated when the stimulus is next encountered. Stimulus control is a critical aspect of shaping and maintaining the behaviors we observe in both humans and animals.

***

Behavior Chains

A behavior chain is a series of discrete responses or behaviors that are linked together to produce a final outcome. Each response or behavior in the chain is both the consequence of the previous behavior and the stimulus for the next behavior. This process is often used when teaching complex tasks that can be divided into a sequence of smaller steps or actions.

Imagine teaching a child to tie their shoes. This task can be broken down into a chain of behaviors:

1. Crossing the laces.

2. Tucking one lace under the other.

3. Pulling both laces tight.

4. Forming loops with both laces.

5. Crossing the loops.

6. Tucking one loop under the other.

7. Pulling the loops tight to complete the knot.

Each step is taught and mastered before moving on to the next, and successful completion of one step acts as a cue for the next step. Mastery of the entire chain results in the ability to tie shoes independently.

Shaping

Shaping, on the other hand, is a method of gradually teaching a new behavior through reinforcement of successive approximations toward the desired behavior. In shaping, you reinforce behaviors that are increasingly similar to the one you want to teach, and you do not reinforce those that are less similar.

Let's take an example of shaping behavior in an animal, such as training a dog to fetch a ball:

1. First, you might reinforce the dog for looking at the ball.

2. Then, you only reinforce when the dog moves toward the ball.

3. Next, the reinforcement comes when the dog touches the ball.

4. Following that, you reinforce the dog for picking up the ball.

5. Finally, the dog receives reinforcement for bringing the ball back to you.

Each step is a closer approximation to the final desired behavior, and the dog is only reinforced for completing the step that is currently being shaped. This way, shaping can help the dog learn a complex behavior that it might not learn on its own.

Both behavior chains and shaping rely on the principle of reinforcement. With behavior chains, the reinforcement is built into the completion of each step leading to the final behavior. With shaping, reinforcement is delivered strategically at each stage of approximation towards the final behavior. These techniques are used widely in teaching new skills, animal training, rehabilitation, and behavior modification programs. They are valuable tools because they allow for the learning of complex behaviors without overwhelming the learner by expecting the final behavior to occur all at once.

***

Generalization and discrimination are two fundamental concepts in behavior analysis that describe how behaviors are applied across different situations or how they are controlled by specific stimuli.

Generalization

Generalization refers to the process by which a behavior that has been learned in one situation occurs in other situations, even though those situations have never been associated with the behavior. In other words, it's the spreading of the effects of learning. The ability to generalize is important because it allows individuals to apply what they've learned in new and varied contexts without having to learn from scratch each time.

For example, if a child learns to say "thank you" when given a toy by their parent, generalization would occur if the child also says "thank you" when a teacher hands them a book, or when a stranger gives them a compliment. The phrase "thank you" has been generalized to different scenarios of receiving something, not just the specific instance with the parent and the toy.

Discrimination

Discrimination, on the other hand, is the process of responding differently in the presence of different stimuli or situations. It involves the ability to distinguish between situations where a behavior should occur and situations where it should not. Discrimination is crucial because it helps individuals to behave appropriately according to the specific nuances of different contexts.

An example of discrimination could involve a child learning that it is okay to shout and be lively on a playground, but not in a library. The child discriminates between the two settings and adjusts their behavior accordingly—the loud, exuberant behavior is emitted in the context of the playground (where it is appropriate) but not in the library (where quiet is expected).

Real-life applications of generalization and discrimination are found in educational settings, clinical interventions, and everyday learning. Teachers and therapists often aim to teach skills that will generalize to various contexts (like social skills or academic knowledge), but they also need to ensure that individuals can discriminate when certain behaviors are appropriate and when they are not (like understanding social cues or situational norms).

For a behavior to be considered truly learned and functional, it often needs to be both generalizable across relevant situations and discriminable when the context demands specific responses. Balancing these two aspects is a central goal in many behavioral training and intervention programs.

Here are some real-life examples of generalization and discrimination:

Generalization Examples

1. **Learning to Drive:** Once you've learned to drive one car, you can generally operate another car without relearning everything. The skills you've acquired are generalized to different vehicles, although they might have some differences in controls.

2. **Greeting People:** If you're taught to shake hands as a greeting in a social context, you might generalize this behavior and offer your hand when meeting someone new in a professional setting as well.

3. **Customer Service Skills:** A barista trained at one coffee shop can generalize their customer service skills when they start working at a different cafe. The ability to interact with customers, take orders, and manage payments is not limited to just one location.

Discrimination Examples

1. **Classroom Behavior:** A student learns to speak out loud in class when they have a question but also learns to stay quiet during a test. They discriminate between interactive class time and quiet test time.

2. **Work vs. Home Clothes:** An individual wears formal attire to a corporate job but changes into casual clothes at home. They discriminate between the appropriate dress code for work and for leisure time at home.

3. **Pet Training:** A dog is trained to urinate outside in the yard but understands not to do so inside the house. The dog discriminates between locations that are appropriate for relieving itself.

Combination of Generalization and Discrimination:

1. **Using a Smartphone:** Once you learn to text on one smartphone, you can typically apply that skill to different smartphones (generalization). However, you also learn that typing style and language may need to be adjusted depending on whether you're texting a friend or a work colleague (discrimination).

2. **Emergency Responses:** A person who has learned to dial 911 in an emergency can generalize this action to any phone. However, they discriminate by understanding that this number is only to be used in actual emergencies and not for non-emergency situations.

These examples illustrate how generalization and discrimination help individuals navigate the world more efficiently, applying learned behaviors to new contexts, while also distinguishing when certain behaviors are appropriate.

Chapter Five

Assessment in Behavior Analysis

Functional assessments are an integral part of behavior analysis, providing insight into why an individual might engage in certain behaviors, particularly those that are challenging or disruptive. The assessment is like a detective's investigation, involving several methods to uncover the reasons behind a behavior.

1. **Interviews and Questionnaires**: These are used to gather qualitative data from people who interact with the individual regularly. It's like collecting witness statements to understand the context of the behavior.

2. **Direct Observation**: Observing the individual in their natural environment allows for an objective look at the behavior and its antecedents and consequences. It's akin to a detective being on stakeout, looking for patterns or triggers.

3. **Data Collection**: Keeping track of when, where, and how often the behavior occurs. It's the gathering of evidence, noting down everything from the environment to the individual's response to different situations.

4. **Hypothesis Development**: Based on the evidence gathered, forming a hypothesis about the function of the behavior is like creating a theory that ties together all the clues.

5. **Functional Analysis**: This is the testing phase, where the environment is manipulated to see if the behavior changes accordingly. It confirms or refutes the hypothesis, much like a detective setting a trap to catch the culprit.

Through these steps, behavior analysts aim to understand the function of a behavior, which could be to gain attention, escape a task, get access to tangible items, or satisfy sensory needs. With this understanding, they can then develop tailored interventions that address these functions, ultimately helping the individual to replace challenging behaviors with more appropriate ones.

Imagine a student who frequently disrupts the class by calling out without raising their hand. A behavior analyst is called to conduct a functional assessment. They would first interview the teacher, parents, and possibly the student to gather initial observations about the behavior. Then, they would observe the student in the classroom setting, taking note of what happens immediately before and after the behavior occurs.

Through these observations, the analyst might notice that the student tends to call out during math instruction and that following these outbursts, the teacher provides one-on-one attention to assist the student. With this information, the analyst might hypothesize that the function of the student's behavior is to seek attention.

To test this hypothesis, the behavior analyst may conduct a functional analysis by manipulating the environment. For example, they might arrange conditions where the teacher ignores the outbursts (to test if the behavior is maintained without attention) and conditions where the student receives regular attention (to see if the behavior reduces when attention is freely available).

If the student calls out less when attention is given freely, it supports the hypothesis that the behavior is maintained by social attention. The analyst can then recommend an intervention, such as teaching the student to ask for help appropriately or altering the instruction method to be more engaging, thus reducing the need for the student to seek attention through calling out.

***

Identifying and Defining Target Behaviors

In behavior analysis, identifying and defining target behaviors is a meticulous process that involves specifying exactly what the individual will do or say that constitutes a particular behavior of interest. This is crucial because it sets the foundation for accurate measurement, assessment, and intervention.

Here's a detailed look into this process:

1. **Operational Definition**: The behavior must be defined in a clear, observable, and measurable way. It should be so precise that different observers can recognize and record the behavior consistently. For example, instead of saying "aggression," you would define it as "strikes out with hand or foot, making contact with others."

2. **Measurable Components**: You'll need to identify the dimensions of the behavior that can be measured—frequency, duration, intensity, or latency. For instance, if the target behavior is 'completing homework,' you might measure how often homework is completed on time, how long it takes to finish, or the accuracy of the completed work.

3. **Relevance of the Behavior**: The behavior chosen should be socially significant and directly impact the individual's life. This means focusing on behaviors that will improve the individual's quality of life or reduce harm.

4. **Context**: The behavior should be defined in the context in which it occurs because the environment can affect how and when the behavior is exhibited.

5. **Functionality**: The target behavior should have a function for the individual. Understanding why an individual engages in a behavior (for attention, escape, sensory stimulation, etc.) can guide how it is addressed.

6. **Generality**: The target behavior should be defined in a way that encourages generalization—meaning the behavior should be useful in a variety of settings and continue over time.

By thoroughly identifying and defining target behaviors, behavior analysts can ensure that their interventions are focused, relevant, and effective.

For each of the components in identifying and defining target behaviors, here are examples:

1. **Operational Definition**: If the target behavior is "participating in class," an operational definition might be "raising a hand and waiting to be called on before speaking."
2. **Measurable Components**: For "completing homework," you might measure frequency (e.g., "completes homework 5 out of 5 school nights"), duration (e.g., "spends at least 30 minutes on homework daily"), and accuracy (e.g., "scores at least 90% correct on homework assignments").
3. **Relevance of the Behavior**: Teaching a child to request items they want instead of screaming; the behavior is relevant as it promotes communication and reduces disruptive outbursts.
4. **Context**: A student may exhibit disruptive behavior, such as "yelling out answers," more frequently in a large group setting than during one-on-one instruction.
5. **Functionality**: If a child screams to escape an undesired activity, teaching them to use a "break" card instead offers a functional alternative.
6. **Generality**: A student is taught to greet peers with "Hello" and use this behavior across various social settings, such as school, sports teams, or group outings.

***

Data Collection Methods

Data collection is a cornerstone of behavior analysis, allowing for objective and systematic recording of behaviors to assess and monitor progress. Here are several methods commonly used:

1. **Frequency/Event Recording**: Tallying each time a behavior occurs. It's useful for behaviors with a clear start and end.

2. **Duration Recording**: Measuring the amount of time a behavior lasts. This method is particularly useful for behaviors you want to increase or decrease in length.

3. **Interval Recording**: Dividing observation time into intervals and recording if the behavior occurred during each interval. It can be partial or whole interval recording.

4. **Time Sampling**: Similar to interval recording but involves noting if the behavior occurs at specific points in time, such as every 10 minutes.

5. **Latency Recording**: Measuring the time that elapses between a specific event or instruction and the start of the behavior.

6. **ABC Data Collection**: Recording the Antecedent (what happens before the behavior), the Behavior itself, and the Consequence (what happens after the behavior).

7. **Permanent Product Recording**: Measuring behaviors that have a clear outcome or result that can be seen even after the behavior has stopped.

Each of these methods has its place depending on the behavior being measured and the goals of the assessment. They provide a rich data set that can be analyzed to understand patterns and effects of interventions over time.

Here are examples for each data collection method:

1. **Frequency/Event Recording**: Counting how many times a student raises their hand in class during a day.

2. **Duration Recording**: Timing how long a child plays with a toy without interruption.

3. **Interval Recording**: Checking every 5 minutes to see if a patient is engaging in a repetitive behavior during a therapy session.

4. **Time Sampling**: Observing a student at random times to note if they are on-task or off-task.

5. **Latency Recording**: Measuring the time from the teacher's instruction to begin a task to the student's initiation of the task.

6. **ABC Data Collection**: Noting what happened immediately before a child's tantrum (antecedent), describing the tantrum behavior, and what occurred as a result (consequence), such as being given a toy.

7. **Permanent Product Recording**: Grading a set of math problems completed by a student to assess their calculation skills.

***

Analyzing Behavioral Data

Analyzing behavioral data involves interpreting the information collected during observation and measurement of the target behavior. Here's a broad overview of how this data might be analyzed:

1. **Graphing**: Data is often plotted on a graph to visually display patterns over time. This can include line graphs for frequency and duration, or bar graphs for comparing different conditions.

2. **Trend Analysis**: Looking at the direction of the data path on a graph to determine if the behavior is increasing, decreasing, or staying the same over time.

3. **Level**: Determining the average level of the behavior across a given time frame, such as the daily frequency of a behavior over a week.

4. **Variability**: Examining how much the behavior fluctuates during the observation period.

5. **Comparative Analysis**: If an intervention is in place, comparing data from before and after the intervention to determine its impact.

The goal is to use this analysis to make informed decisions about behavioral interventions and their effectiveness.

Here are examples for each data analysis technique:

1. **Graphing**: A behavior analyst may plot the number of times a student calls out in class on a line graph to show changes over the course of a school term.
2. **Trend Analysis**: If a graph shows a consistent downward slope in the line representing outbursts over several weeks, this indicates a decreasing trend in the behavior.
3. **Level**: After implementing a new teaching strategy, the analyst calculates the average number of homework assignments completed per week to determine the level of the behavior.
4. **Variability**: The analyst observes that the frequency of a child's tantrums varies significantly from day to day, indicating high variability and potentially influencing the choice of intervention strategies.
5. **Comparative Analysis**: Comparing the rate of a target behavior before and after the introduction of a reward system, the analyst may find that the behavior increased significantly post-intervention, suggesting the effectiveness of the strategy.

Chapter Six

Behavior Change Procedures

Selection and implementation of interventions in behavior change procedures involve a systematic process to choose and apply strategies that are expected to modify the target behavior. Here are real-life examples for each step:

1. **Identify the Target Behavior**: Clearly define the behavior that needs to be changed. For example, a teacher may want to increase a student's on-task behavior in the classroom.

2. **Selecting the Intervention**: Based on the functional assessment, the behavior analyst may choose an intervention. For instance, if off-task behavior is maintained by escape from difficult tasks, the intervention might include breaking tasks down into smaller, more manageable parts.

3. **Implementing the Intervention**: The chosen intervention is put into practice. Using the previous example, the teacher would begin giving shorter assignments to the student to encourage completion.

4. **Monitoring Progress**: The effectiveness of the intervention is regularly assessed by collecting data on the target behavior. If the student starts to complete more assignments, this indicates that the intervention may be working.

5. **Modifying Interventions Based on Data**: If progress monitoring shows that the intervention is not effective, it may need to be adjusted. For instance, if the student is still not completing assignments, the teacher might implement

additional strategies, like a reward system for completed work.

6. **Generalization and Maintenance**: Once the intervention is successful, plans are made for the student to maintain the behavior over time and generalize it to other settings or tasks.

7. **Stakeholder Training and Involvement**: Parents, teachers, and other stakeholders are trained to support the intervention to ensure consistency across different environments.

8. **Ethical Considerations**: All interventions should be selected and implemented with consideration of the individual's rights and best interests, following ethical guidelines.

Each of these steps requires careful planning and continuous data analysis to ensure that the interventions are effective and ethical.

Here are examples of each step in the selection and implementation of behavior change interventions:

1. **Identifying the Target Behavior**: A parent wants to reduce the number of tantrums their child has in public settings.

2. **Selecting the Intervention**: After a functional assessment, the parent, guided by a behavior analyst, decides to use a visual schedule to prepare the child for transitions, which often trigger tantrums.

3. **Implementing the Intervention**: The visual schedule is introduced to the child, and the parent uses it consistently before each outing to show the sequence of activities.

4. **Monitoring Progress**: The parent keeps a log of the number of tantrums per week to see if there is a decrease after introducing the visual schedule.

5. **Modifying Interventions Based on Data**: If no change is observed, the behavior analyst might suggest adding a token system to reinforce calm behavior.

6. **Generalization and Maintenance**: Once tantrums decrease, the parent works

on using the strategies in various public settings to generalize the calm behavior.

7. **Stakeholder Training and Involvement**: The behavior analyst trains the child's school staff on using the visual schedule to support the child during transitions at school.

8. **Ethical Considerations**: Throughout the process, the analyst ensures the child's dignity is respected, and all strategies are in the child's best interest.

***

Crisis Management Techniques

Crisis management techniques are strategies used to deal with sudden and significant negative events. Here are some examples:

1. **De-escalation Techniques**: Using calm, non-threatening body language and a soothing tone of voice to reduce the intensity of the situation.

2. **Safety Interventions**: Removing any immediate physical threats to the individual or others, and ensuring a safe environment.

3. **Emergency Interventions**: In situations where there is a risk of harm, trained professionals may need to use emergency interventions like physical holds, which must be done following strict guidelines to ensure safety.

4. **Supportive Listening**: Providing an attentive ear and acknowledging the individual's feelings without judgment can often alleviate the immediate crisis.

5. **Problem-Solving**: Assisting the individual in identifying the problem and brainstorming potential solutions.

6. **Follow-Up Care**: Ensuring the individual receives ongoing support following the crisis, which may include counseling or therapy.

7. **Training and Preparation**: Regularly training staff in crisis intervention techniques to prepare them for potential situations.

8. **Postvention**: After a crisis, analyzing what happened, providing support to those affected, and revising policies or procedures as necessary.

It's essential to handle crises ethically and safely, always prioritizing the well-being of the individual involved.

let's delve into each crisis management technique with detailed examples:

1. **De-escalation Techniques**
    - **Example**: Imagine a high school student becomes agitated and starts yelling in the classroom, knocking books off a desk. A teacher might approach calmly, maintaining a non-confrontational stance, and speak in a low, soothing tone. The teacher could say, "I see you're really upset right now, and that's okay. Let's go outside for a moment and talk about it, away from the classroom noise."
2. **Safety Interventions**
    - **Example**: In a mental health facility, if a patient becomes physically aggressive, the staff might first clear the area of any objects that could be used as weapons. They might also guide other patients to a different area to prevent harm.
3. **Emergency Interventions**
    - **Example**: In extreme cases where a person might be a danger to themselves or others, and all other de-escalation strategies have failed, professionals might need to employ emergency interventions. For instance, a team trained in safe restraint techniques might gently but firmly hold the individual to prevent harm until they can be assessed by medical personnel.
4. **Supportive Listening**
    - **Example**: During a crisis hotline call, the responder might use phrases like, "It sounds like you're in a lot of pain right now," or "I'm here with you, and I want to understand what you're going through," to validate the caller's feelings and build a rapport.

5. **Problem-Solving**
   - **Example**: A manager notices an employee showing signs of extreme stress due to workload. The manager might sit down with the employee to discuss what tasks are most pressing and help the employee create a more manageable schedule or delegate tasks.
6. **Follow-Up Care**
   - **Example**: After a student experiences a crisis at school, such as a panic attack, the school counselor might schedule regular check-ins with the student to provide emotional support and might also refer the student to a therapist for ongoing care.
7. **Training and Preparation**
   - **Example**: A hospital regularly conducts training sessions for staff on how to recognize signs of a patient in distress and how to perform CPI (Crisis Prevention Intervention). They might run simulated scenarios where staff can practice these skills in a controlled environment.
8. **Postvention**
   - **Example**: After an incident where emergency services had to be called to a group home due to a violent outburst, the management conducts a debriefing session. In this session, they discuss what led to the outburst, how it was handled, and what could be done differently in the future to prevent such incidents. They might also offer counseling sessions for residents and staff who were affected by the event.

In all these examples, the key elements include maintaining safety, using effective communication, providing support, and ensuring any interventions are proportionate to the situation and conducted ethically. The focus is always on minimizing harm and supporting the individual in crisis to regain a sense of control and safety.

***

Ethical Considerations in Intervention

Ethical considerations are critical in the implementation of interventions, especially in the field of behavior analysis or any situation where there is an intervention in human behavior. Here are some key principles and examples:

1. **Informed Consent**
   - **Example**: Before starting a new therapy program for individuals with developmental disabilities, practitioners must obtain informed consent from the individuals or their guardians, clearly explaining the nature of the treatment, potential risks, and benefits.
2. **Right to Effective Treatment**
   - **Example**: A school that adopts a new behavioral intervention must ensure that the program is based on evidence and research, thus offering the most effective known treatment for its students with behavioral challenges.
3. **Confidentiality**
   - **Example**: In a clinical setting, therapists must keep all client information private and only share details with others as allowed by the client or legal requirements, ensuring that discussions, records, and treatment details are securely handled.
4. **Professional Boundaries**
   - **Example**: A therapist working with a vulnerable adult maintains a professional relationship and avoids dual relationships that could impair objectivity, such as becoming personal friends or entering into a business relationship with the client.
5. **Beneficence and Nonmaleficence**
   - **Example**: When choosing an intervention, a clinician must consider the welfare of the client first, ensuring the selected treatment will benefit the client without causing harm, and if any risk is involved, it must be out-

weighed by the potential benefits.

6. **Accountability and Evaluation**

   - **Example**: After implementing a new behavior plan in a residential treatment facility, staff must regularly evaluate the effectiveness of the intervention, making adjustments as necessary, and are accountable for the outcomes of their clients.

7. **Cultural Competence**

   - **Example**: Interventions must be culturally sensitive and appropriate. A behavior analyst working with families from diverse backgrounds takes time to understand cultural norms and values before designing and implementing interventions.

8. **Consent and Assent**

   - **Example**: While working with children, practitioners not only obtain consent from the parents but also seek the assent of the child, explaining the treatment in age-appropriate language and respecting the child's willingness to participate.

9. **Least Restrictive Procedures**

   - **Example**: In a case where a client exhibits self-injurious behavior, the intervention plan starts with the least restrictive options, such as positive reinforcement for alternative behaviors, before considering more intrusive or restrictive methods.

10. **Transparency**

    - **Example**: A practitioner openly communicates with the client about the goals and methods of treatment, and any data collected is shared with the client or their legal representatives, ensuring transparency in the entire process.

These ethical principles guide practitioners to conduct themselves professionally and respectfully, with the client's rights and well-being at the forefront of any intervention.

Chapter Seven

Supervision and Management

The Board Certified Behavior Analyst (BCBA) plays a crucial role in supervising and managing the delivery of applied behavior analysis (ABA) services. Below are some of the key roles and responsibilities of a BCBA:

1. **Assessment and Evaluation**: BCBAs conduct comprehensive assessments to identify the functions of behaviors and determine the necessity for behavior-analytic services. This might involve using tools like the Functional Behavior Assessment (FBA) or the Verbal Behavior Milestones Assessment and Placement Program (VB-MAPP).

2. **Designing and Implementing Interventions**: They create individualized intervention plans based on assessment results. The BCBA ensures that interventions are evidence-based and tailored to the client's needs.

3. **Data Analysis**: BCBAs are responsible for ensuring that data collection methods are implemented consistently. They analyze the collected data to monitor progress and make necessary adjustments to the intervention plan.

4. **Training and Supervision**: A significant part of a BCBA's role involves training, supervising, and providing ongoing guidance to Registered Behavior Technicians (RBTs), BCBA candidates, and other staff implementing behavior-analytic interventions.

5. **Ethical Conduct**: They must adhere to the ethical guidelines set out by the

Behavior Analyst Certification Board (BACB). This includes maintaining confidentiality, practicing within one's scope of competence, and ensuring that all interventions are in the best interest of the client.

6. **Consultation**: BCBAs often act as consultants in various settings, such as schools, homes, and community agencies, providing expert guidance on behavior-analytic practices.

7. **Collaboration**: They collaborate with other professionals, such as teachers, psychologists, and occupational therapists, to ensure a comprehensive approach to the client's development and well-being.

8. **Advocacy**: BCBAs advocate for the appropriate use of ABA principles and techniques and may also work to increase access to ABA services in underserved communities or populations.

9. **Professional Development**: They are responsible for their own ongoing professional development, staying current with research and best practices in the field of behavior analysis.

10. **Documentation and Reporting**: BCBAs are tasked with maintaining accurate records of assessments, treatment plans, progress reports, and other documentation related to the services provided.

11. **Program Evaluation**: They routinely evaluate the effectiveness of the ABA programs they oversee and make data-driven decisions regarding program continuation, modification, or termination.

12. **Communication**: BCBAs maintain clear and professional communication with clients, caregivers, and other stakeholders to discuss progress, concerns, and any changes to the intervention plans.

By fulfilling these roles and responsibilities, BCBAs ensure high-quality, ethical, and effective delivery of ABA services to their clients.

here are examples for each of the roles and responsibilities of a Board Certified Behavior Analyst (BCBA):

1. **Assessment and Evaluation**:
   - A BCBA may use the Functional Behavior Assessment (FBA) to determine why a child with autism engages in self-injurious behavior. The assessment could reveal that the behavior occurs more frequently when the child is asked to do a difficult task, suggesting the behavior is a form of escape from demanding situations.
2. **Designing and Implementing Interventions**:
   - After identifying that a child bites their hand to escape tasks, a BCBA designs an intervention where the child is taught to request a break using a picture exchange system. This intervention replaces the harmful behavior with a more appropriate communication method.
3. **Data Analysis**:
   - The BCBA regularly reviews the frequency of hand-biting incidents recorded by the RBT during sessions. They notice a decrease in hand-biting when the picture exchange system is consistently used and decide to continue with this intervention while monitoring for further improvement.
4. **Training and Supervision**:
   - A BCBA conducts a workshop for RBTs on implementing discrete trial training (DTT) effectively. They observe the RBTs during sessions, provide feedback, and ensure fidelity to the intervention protocols.
5. **Ethical Conduct**:
   - An ethical dilemma arises when a school asks the BCBA to use a technique not supported by ABA principles. The BCBA refuses and explains the importance of using evidence-based practices, adhering to the BACB's ethical guidelines.
6. **Consultation**:
   - A BCBA consults with a local clinic to develop a feeding program for children with food aversions. They work with occupational therapists to

create a multidisciplinary approach to treatment.

7. **Collaboration**:
    - During an Individualized Education Program (IEP) meeting, the BCBA collaborates with teachers, parents, and the school psychologist to integrate behavior goals and ABA strategies into the student's educational plan.
8. **Advocacy**:
    - A BCBA may advocate for insurance coverage of ABA services by presenting data on the effectiveness of ABA to policymakers or insurance companies.
9. **Professional Development**:
    - The BCBA attends a conference on the latest research in ABA and the treatment of severe behavior disorders to ensure they are using the most current and effective practices.
10. **Documentation and Reporting**:
    - After each session, the BCBA writes progress notes detailing the client's responses to interventions, adjusts the treatment plan as necessary, and prepares reports for caregivers and insurance providers.
11. **Program Evaluation**:
    - The BCBA analyzes long-term data on a student's progress in reducing aggressive behavior. They adjust the behavior intervention plan to phase out prompts as the student gains more independence in managing their behavior.
12. **Communication**:
    - The BCBA holds a meeting with the parents of a child to discuss the child's progress, address any concerns, and plan for generalizing skills from the therapy setting to the home environment.

These examples illustrate how BCBAs apply their knowledge and skills in various practical situations, always aiming to improve the quality of life for the individuals they serve.

***

Effective Supervision Practices

Effective supervision practices for a BCBA (Board Certified Behavior Analyst) might include the following examples:

1. **Behavioral Skills Training (BST)**:
    - This involves several steps. First, the BCBA would provide a clear and concise description of the skill to be learned. They would then model the skill in a role-playing scenario or in a real-life context. The supervisee would practice the skill (rehearsal) while the BCBA observes and collects data on their performance. Finally, the BCBA would provide immediate feedback, highlighting what was done well and what needs improvement. This cycle continues until the supervisee demonstrates mastery.
2. **Performance Monitoring**:
    - Performance monitoring is a data-driven approach. The BCBA reviews the supervisee's written records and observes their performance directly. The BCBA would look for consistency between the supervisee's actions and the treatment plan, check the reliability of data collection, and ensure adherence to protocols. Regular meetings to review these findings help keep the supervisee informed about areas needing attention and reinforce good practices.
3. **Ongoing Professional Development**:
    - Continuous education is vital in a field that is constantly evolving with new research and strategies. The BCBA could facilitate journal clubs where recent articles are discussed, or they might arrange for external experts to deliver workshops. Supervisees might also be encouraged to present case studies to their peers, fostering a collaborative learning environment.

4. **Feedback Systems**:
    - Feedback should be systematic and frequent. It could be structured as weekly one-on-one meetings or written feedback forms after observing a session. The feedback should be specific, objective, and delivered in a supportive manner. A good practice is to start with positive feedback before moving on to areas for improvement to maintain a positive and constructive atmosphere.
5. **Ethical Considerations**:
    - Supervisees must be well-versed in the ethical standards of the profession. The BCBA might use role-playing scenarios to simulate ethical dilemmas and guide the supervisee through the decision-making process. Discussions could also include case studies where ethical concerns were present, and how they were resolved.
6. **Goal Setting and Evaluation**:
    - The BCBA and supervisee could set professional development goals using the SMART criteria. These goals are then revisited in regular intervals to assess progress and make adjustments if needed. This process ensures that the supervisee is making continuous progress and that supervision is targeted and effective.
7. **Modeling**:
    - By consistently displaying professional behavior, the BCBA sets the standard for the supervisee. This includes demonstrating how to interact with clients, how to manage challenging behaviors, and how to apply ABA principles in practice. The BCBA's actions provide a live template for the supervisee to emulate.
8. **Supportive Environment**:
    - A supportive environment is one where supervisees feel valued and understood. The BCBA should foster open communication, encourage questions, and create a non-judgmental space for discussing mistakes. This can

build trust and allow for more effective learning and professional growth.

9. **Individualized Supervision**:
   - Just as interventions are individualized for clients, supervision should be tailored to the supervisee's needs. This might mean adjusting the level of support, changing the focus of supervision sessions, or providing different resources depending on the supervisee's strengths and areas for growth.
10. **Documentation and Record-Keeping**:
    - Good record-keeping is essential for accountability and for tracking the supervisee's journey. Detailed records of meetings, goals, feedback, and outcomes are important for evaluating the effectiveness of supervision and can be useful for credentialing and auditing purposes.
11. **Cultural Competency**:
    - Cultural competency ensures that services are respectful of and responsive to the health beliefs, practices, and cultural and linguistic needs of diverse clients. The BCBA might include training on cultural sensitivity, discussing cultural influences on behavior, and encouraging supervisees to reflect on their cultural competence regularly.
12. **Peer Review and Consultation**:
    - Engaging with peers in reviewing each other's work can provide new perspectives and insights. The BCBA might facilitate case conferences where supervisees present their cases and receive feedback from their peers, fostering a collaborative and reflective practice culture.

Through these practices, a BCBA ensures that the supervision they provide is not only effective in developing the skills of their supervisees but also in enhancing the quality of service to clients and adhering to the professional and ethical standards of the field.

Here are examples of each of the effective supervision practices for a Board Certified Behavior Analyst (BCBA):

1. **Behavioral Skills Training (BST)**:

- Example: A BCBA is supervising a new therapist on how to implement discrete trial training (DTT) with a client. The BCBA explains the steps, models the procedure, observes the therapist practicing with a client, and then provides feedback.

2. **Performance Monitoring**:

    - Example: The BCBA reviews video recordings of therapy sessions conducted by the supervisee and checks the accuracy of their data collection against the video to ensure the supervisee is correctly implementing the intervention plan.

3. **Ongoing Professional Development**:

    - Example: The BCBA organizes a monthly in-service training where all staff members present on a recent research article related to ABA therapy to stay informed about the latest evidence-based practices.

4. **Feedback Systems**:

    - Example: The BCBA sets up a bi-weekly review session with the supervisee where they discuss case progress, review the supervisee's performance, and provide both commendations and recommendations for improvement.

5. **Ethical Considerations**:

    - Example: The BCBA presents hypothetical scenarios that may present ethical dilemmas, such as dual relationships or confidentiality breaches, and discusses with the supervisee how to handle these situations according to the Professional and Ethical Compliance Code for Behavior Analysts.

6. **Goal Setting and Evaluation**:

    - Example: The BCBA works with the supervisee to set specific goals such as mastering a certain number of ABA techniques within three months. They then review these goals quarterly to evaluate the supervisee's progress and provide guidance on areas that need additional focus.

7. **Modeling**:

- Example: The BCBA demonstrates how to conduct a functional behavior assessment (FBA) while the supervisee observes. This modeling helps the supervisee learn the proper way to conduct an FBA through observation.

8. **Supportive Environment**:
   - Example: The BCBA creates a group chat for all supervisees where they can share experiences, ask questions, and seek support from each other, fostering a team environment.

9. **Individualized Supervision**:
   - Example: The BCBA notices a supervisee struggling with managing aggressive behavior in clients, so they focus several supervision sessions specifically on behavior de-escalation techniques tailored to the supervisee's needs.

10. **Documentation and Record-Keeping**:
    - Example: The BCBA instructs the supervisee in maintaining accurate records of all sessions, including notes on client progress and specific interventions used, which are regularly reviewed during supervision meetings.

11. **Cultural Competency**:
    - Example: The BCBA assigns the supervisee to work with a family from a different cultural background and provides resources and training on cultural sensitivity to ensure the supervisee can effectively communicate and respect the family's values and beliefs.

12. **Peer Review and Consultation**:
    - Example: The BCBA organizes monthly case conferences where supervisees present challenging cases to their colleagues and discuss different strategies for intervention, providing an opportunity for peer consultation and collaborative problem-solving.

These examples illustrate how BCBAs can implement each of these effective supervision practices to foster professional growth, ensure high-quality service delivery, and maintain ethical standards in their supervisees' practice.

***

Staff Training and Performance Management

For effective staff training and performance management, it's crucial that the procedures are not just implemented but are brought to life through daily practice. Here is an elaboration on the examples:

1. **Developing Training Programs**:
    - A BCBA may create a curriculum that includes a mixture of theoretical learning, practical demonstrations, and supervised practice, ensuring that new therapists have both the knowledge and skills needed to deliver high-quality ABA therapy.
2. **Competency-Based Training**:
    - Staff might undergo a structured series of training stages, where they demonstrate increasing levels of skill across different ABA techniques. They might start with basic skills like data collection and gradually work up to more complex tasks like implementing behavior intervention plans.
3. **Performance Feedback**:
    - After each observation, the BCBA could use a standardized feedback form that highlights what the staff member did well and what needs improvement. This form could include a scoring system to help staff track their progress over time.
4. **Data-Driven Performance Management**:
    - The BCBA might graph staff performance metrics and review these during supervision meetings. They could analyze trends and discuss strategies for improvement, making the process transparent and collaborative.
5. **Continuous Monitoring**:

- The BCBA could establish regular check-ins and spot observations, sometimes unannounced, to ensure that staff members maintain a high standard of practice at all times, and to provide on-the-spot coaching as needed.

6. **Skill Generalization and Maintenance**:
   - To promote skill maintenance, the BCBA may introduce simulated scenarios or role-playing exercises during staff meetings, allowing staff to practice and refine their skills in a controlled, supportive environment.

7. **Goal-Setting for Staff Development**:
   - During one-on-one meetings, the BCBA and staff members might set professional development targets and discuss strategies for achieving them, ensuring that each staff member has a clear path for career advancement.

8. **Incentives and Motivation Systems**:
   - A BCBA might set up a 'therapist of the month' program that rewards staff who exemplify excellent clinical practice and who have made significant contributions to client progress.

9. **Crisis Management and De-escalation Training**:
   - BCBAs could conduct bi-annual workshops that use role-play and other interactive methods to train staff on managing challenging behaviors and emergencies effectively and safely.

10. **Ethical Training and Compliance**:
    - Ethical training may include case studies and discussions about how to navigate complex situations, reinforcing the importance of ethical behavior in every aspect of the job.

11. **Creating a Culture of Feedback**:
    - The BCBA might introduce regular 'roundtable' discussions where staff can share experiences and provide each other with peer feedback in a structured, supportive setting.

12. **Leadership Development**:
    - Potential leaders may be given the opportunity to lead team meetings, manage small projects, or mentor new staff under the guidance of the BCBA, providing them with practical leadership experience.

In all these ways, the BCBA ensures that the training and management of staff are not just a formality but a dynamic and integral part of the service delivery, aiming to foster a high-performing team that delivers consistent, ethical, and effective ABA services.

Here are some detailed examples of how a Board Certified Behavior Analyst (BCBA) might approach this aspect of their work:

1. **Developing Training Programs**:
    - **Example**: A BCBA creates a comprehensive onboarding program for new hires that includes modules on Applied Behavior Analysis (ABA) principles, specific intervention strategies, data collection methods, and safety protocols. This program combines online learning with hands-on practice sessions.
2. **Competency-Based Training**:
    - **Example**: The BCBA sets up a series of assessments to measure staff competency in key areas such as implementing reinforcement schedules, conducting discrete trial training, and managing challenging behaviors. Staff members are required to demonstrate proficiency in these areas before working independently with clients.
3. **Performance Feedback**:
    - **Example**: After observing a staff member conduct a therapy session, the BCBA provides specific, constructive feedback on their performance. This might include praise for correctly implemented strategies and suggestions for areas of improvement, such as timing of reinforcement or accuracy of data recording.
4. **Data-Driven Performance Management**:

- **Example**: The BCBA uses data from therapy sessions to analyze staff performance trends. For instance, they might track the frequency of correct prompt fading over time, using this data to inform decisions about additional training or support needed.

5. **Continuous Monitoring**:

    - **Example**: The BCBA regularly schedules direct observation and co-treatment sessions with staff to continuously monitor their application of ABA techniques, ensuring adherence to the treatment plan and identifying areas for ongoing professional development.

6. **Skill Generalization and Maintenance**:

    - **Example**: To ensure that staff can apply their skills across various settings and maintain their competencies over time, the BCBA sets up periodic skill refreshers and cross-contextual training opportunities, such as role-playing different scenarios or working with different client profiles.

7. **Goal-Setting for Staff Development**:

    - **Example**: The BCBA collaborates with staff members to set individual professional development goals, such as mastering a new behavior assessment tool or leading a parent training workshop, and provides resources and support to achieve these goals.

8. **Incentives and Motivation Systems**:

    - **Example**: The BCBA implements a system of incentives for staff to encourage excellent performance. This might include recognition programs, professional development opportunities, or other rewards for meeting or exceeding performance standards.

9. **Crisis Management and De-escalation Training**:

    - **Example**: The BCBA conducts regular training sessions on crisis management, teaching staff de-escalation techniques, and how to apply emergency procedures to ensure the safety of both clients and staff during critical incidents.

10. **Ethical Training and Compliance**:
    - **Example**: The BCBA holds training sessions on ethical considerations, such as confidentiality and professional boundaries, and ensures that staff members understand and comply with the BACB's ethical guidelines.
11. **Creating a Culture of Feedback**:
    - **Example**: The BCBA fosters an environment where staff feel comfortable providing and receiving feedback. This could involve regular team meetings where staff can discuss challenges and successes and give peer-to-peer feedback.
12. **Leadership Development**:
    - **Example**: Recognizing the potential in certain staff members, the BCBA might provide them with additional responsibilities and mentoring to develop their leadership skills, potentially preparing them for supervisory roles in the future.

By focusing on these areas, a BCBA ensures that the staff they manage are well-trained, competent, and motivated, which is essential for providing high-quality ABA services to clients.

Chapter Eight

Ethics in Behavior Analysis

The Professional and Ethical Compliance Code for Behavior Analysts is a set of guidelines developed by the Behavior Analyst Certification Board (BACB). These guidelines are meant to provide behavior analysts with a standard for professional and ethical behavior. It covers a wide range of topics, including:

1. **Responsibility to Clients**: Ensuring the welfare of clients by providing only those services for which the analyst is trained and qualified.

2. **Competence and Service Delivery**: Committing to lifelong learning and providing services based on the best available scientific evidence.

3. **Integrity and Professionalism**: Behavior analysts must be truthful and honest and avoid conflicts of interest.

4. **Confidentiality**: Protecting the privacy of clients and obtaining consent before using any client information for training, research, or other purposes.

5. **Behavior Analysts' Ethical Responsibility to the Field of Behavior Analysis**: Upholding the integrity of the profession by following the code and encouraging colleagues to do the same.

6. **Behavior Analysts' Ethical Responsibility to Colleagues**: Engaging in professional relationships based on the principles of mutual respect, cooperation, and understanding.

7. **Public Statements and Advertising**: Being truthful in public statements and avoiding false or deceptive statements.

This code ensures that behavior analysts act in the best interests of their clients, the profession, and society. It's important for all behavior analysts to familiarize themselves with these ethical standards and integrate them into their professional conduct.

Here are examples for each of the areas mentioned within the Professional and Ethical Compliance Code for Behavior Analysts:

1. **Responsibility to Clients**: A behavior analyst is working with a child with autism. They ensure that the treatment plans are individualized for the child's needs and based on the latest research in applied behavior analysis (ABA). They avoid using outdated or unsupported methods.

2. **Competence and Service Delivery**: An analyst regularly attends workshops and conferences to stay updated with the latest developments in ABA. They apply new, evidence-based practices and interventions that are proven to be effective for the specific populations they serve.

3. **Integrity and Professionalism**: A behavior analyst is offered a kickback for referring clients to a particular service provider. They decline the offer because it is against the ethical code to accept any form of incentive that could create a conflict of interest.

4. **Confidentiality**: Before presenting a case study at a conference, the behavior analyst obtains consent from the client's guardians and ensures that all identifying information is removed or altered to prevent the identification of the client.

5. **Behavior Analysts' Ethical Responsibility to the Field of Behavior Analysis**: Upon noticing that a colleague is employing non-evidence-based practices, a behavior analyst might approach the colleague to discuss the issue and encourage them to review current research and adhere to evidence-based protocols.

6. **Behavior Analysts' Ethical Responsibility to Colleagues**: When disagreements arise between professionals regarding the best approach for a client's treatment, behavior analysts engage in respectful discourse and utilize peer-reviewed research to support their perspectives, fostering an environment of professional growth and collaboration.

7. **Public Statements and Advertising**: In advertising their services, a behavior analyst describes their qualifications accurately and does not make exaggerated claims about the effectiveness of their interventions. They also clearly state their credentials and do not imply they have qualifications or certifications that they do not possess.

These examples illustrate how behavior analysts can apply ethical principles in various professional scenarios to ensure they are acting in a manner consistent with the BACB's ethical guidelines.

***

Ethical Decision-Making Processes

Ethical decision-making processes in behavior analysis involve a structured approach to resolving ethical dilemmas, guided by the Professional and Ethical Compliance Code for Behavior Analysts. Here are some examples of how these processes might be applied in practice:

1. **Consultation with Ethical Codes**: A behavior analyst encounters a situation where they are unsure whether sharing client information with a school is appropriate. The analyst would first consult the BACB's ethical code to determine the guidelines regarding confidentiality and consent.

2. **Seeking Supervision or Consultation**: If the ethical code does not provide a clear answer, the analyst may seek supervision or consultation from a more experienced colleague or an ethics board to discuss the situation and obtain advice on the best course of action.

3. **Evaluating the Rights of All Parties**: The analyst would consider the rights and welfare of the client, ensuring that any decision made respects the client's autonomy, privacy, and legal rights, while also considering the potential benefits and harms to other parties involved, like the school or family.

4. **Considering Multiple Perspectives**: Before making a decision, the analyst

would think about how the decision might impact all stakeholders, including the client, their family, the school system, and the reputation of the field of behavior analysis itself.

5. **Documenting the Decision-Making Process**: The behavior analyst would document the steps taken to resolve the ethical issue, detailing the consultation with the ethical code, discussions with colleagues, and any other resources that were considered.

6. **Evaluating the Outcomes**: After implementing the decision, the analyst would monitor and evaluate the outcomes to ensure that the action taken was beneficial and did not result in unintended negative consequences.

7. **Ongoing Education**: Engaging in continuing education on ethical practices to be prepared for future ethical decision-making and to stay informed about updates to ethical codes and guidelines.

For example, a behavior analyst working with a non-verbal client may consider introducing a new communication device. They would need to weigh the potential benefits of improved communication against the risk of the client relying too heavily on the device, possibly at the expense of developing verbal skills. The analyst would review the ethical code to ensure that the intervention is in the client's best interest, seek advice from knowledgeable colleagues, and carefully document the decision-making process and outcomes.

Here are hypothetical examples of ethical decision-making processes in behavior analysis:

1. **Consulting Ethical Codes**: A BCBA considers whether to accept a gift from a client's family. They refer to the ethical code, which advises against accepting gifts that could influence professional judgment.

2. **Seeking Supervision or Consultation**: Faced with a complex case involving multiple stakeholders, a BCBA seeks advice from a senior colleague to discuss the best course of action that aligns with ethical practices.

3. **Evaluating the Rights of All Parties**: When deciding whether to report a col-

league's unethical behavior, a BCBA weighs the potential harm to the colleague against the duty to the profession and the potential risk to clients.

4. **Considering Multiple Perspectives**: Before transitioning a client out of a successful program, a BCBA considers the perspectives of the client, family, and school staff to ensure the transition is in the client's best interest.
5. **Documenting the Decision-Making Process**: A BCBA keeps detailed records of the decision-making process regarding a client's treatment change, noting the ethical guidelines referenced and the input from all parties involved.
6. **Evaluating the Outcomes**: After implementing a new intervention, the BCBA assesses its effectiveness and ethical implications, ensuring it meets the client's needs without causing harm.
7. **Ongoing Education**: A BCBA attends a workshop on cultural competence to better serve a diverse clientele, reflecting a commitment to ethical practice by acknowledging and respecting cultural differences.

These examples illustrate the application of ethical decision-making processes, ensuring that BCBAs act with integrity and in the best interest of their clients and the profession.

***

Scenarios and Case Studies

Scenarios and case studies are used extensively in behavior analysis to explore ethical dilemmas and complex situations that may not have clear-cut answers. Here are some examples of how they can be utilized:

1. **Role-Playing**: A group of BCBAs might engage in role-playing activities where one plays the client or a family member, and others act as the practitioner facing an ethical dilemma. This could involve a scenario like handling a conflict of interest or addressing dual relationships.
2. **Group Discussion of Hypothetical Cases**: In team meetings, a BCBA may

present a hypothetical case study involving an ethical gray area, such as a client's family requesting non-evidence-based treatments, and facilitate a group discussion on how to handle it.

3. **Analysis of Real-world Situations**: For advanced training, BCBAs might analyze de-identified real-world cases, discussing the interventions used, the outcomes, and whether the ethical standards were upheld throughout the process.

4. **Reflection on Past Experience**: BCBAs can reflect on past cases they have handled, sharing their experiences with others and discussing what they learned, what they might do differently, and how they navigated the ethical aspects of the case.

These activities are instrumental in developing critical thinking, ethical reasoning, and practical decision-making skills among BCBAs. They also help in understanding the complexity of real-life situations and prepare practitioners to handle future ethical challenges more effectively.

Let's delve into each of these with comprehensive examples:

1. **Role-Playing Example**:

    - Scenario: A BCBA is working with a child who has been making significant progress. The parents, impressed with the results, invite the BCBA to their child's birthday party as a guest.

    - Role-Play: One person acts as the BCBA, while others play the role of the parents and colleagues. The 'BCBA' must navigate the situation, considering the ethical implications of attending the party, which may blur professional boundaries.

    - Discussion: The group can discuss potential consequences, like how personal involvement might affect professional judgment or the client's dependence on the therapist. They may also explore alternative responses, such as politely declining while thanking the parents for the invite and suggesting a more appropriate way to celebrate the child's progress within a therapeutic context.

2. **Group Discussion of Hypothetical Cases**:

    - Case: A BCBA is approached by a school to implement a behavior plan for a student. However, the school administration insists on using punitive measures that the BCBA is not comfortable with.

    - Discussion: The BCBA brings this case to their team, and together they discuss the ethical implications of complying with the school's requests versus advocating for evidence-based, non-punitive measures. They weigh the principles of doing no harm, the right to effective treatment, and the potential risks and benefits of each approach.

3. **Analysis of Real-world Situations**:

    - Real-world Situation: A BCBA worked with an adult client with a developmental disability who exhibited self-injurious behavior. A less restrictive intervention was initially tried but was not effective, and the team had to consider a more restrictive option.

    - Analysis: The BCBA presents the case, with all identifying information removed, and discusses the decision-making process that led to the change in intervention. The discussion includes ethical considerations such as the client's right to an effective treatment, the least restrictive environment, and informed consent.

4. **Reflection on Past Experience**:

    - Reflection: A BCBA shares a past experience where they encountered a non-compliant family that refused to follow through with recommended home-based interventions, which led to regression in the client's behavior.

    - Case Study: The BCBA discusses how they addressed the issue by scheduling additional training for the family, setting clearer expectations, and adjusting the intervention to fit the family's context better. The ethical considerations here include respecting the family's autonomy while also advocating for the client's right to effective treatment and the importance of consistency in intervention.

These examples demonstrate the nuanced nature of ethical decision-making in behavior analysis. By engaging with these types of scenarios and case studies, BCBAs can better prepare for the ethical challenges they may face in their professional practice.

Chapter Nine

Exam Preparation Strategies

When preparing for the BCBA exam, creating an effective study schedule and managing your time wisely are crucial steps. Here are examples of how to do this:

1. **Detailed Study Plan Creation**:
   - Outline the entire BCBA task list and allocate specific topics to weeks or days leading up to the exam. For example, dedicate Week 1 to the basic principles of behavior analysis, Week 2 to assessment, and so on.
2. **Time Block Utilization**:
   - Divide each study session into dedicated time blocks focused on different activities: reading, flashcards, practice tests, etc. For instance, within a two-hour study period, spend 50 minutes on reading, 30 minutes on flashcards, and 40 minutes on practice questions.
3. **Goal Setting Per Session**:
   - Define specific outcomes for each study session. For example, "By the end of today's study session, I will be able to list and describe all the schedules of reinforcement and give examples for each."
4. **Task Prioritization Techniques**:
   - Use tools like the Eisenhower Matrix to categorize study tasks by urgency

and importance, focusing first on areas that are both important and urgent.

5. **Break Incorporation Strategies**:
   - Apply scientifically backed techniques like the 52-17 rule, where you focus intensely for 52 minutes and then take a 17-minute break, to maximize productivity.
6. **Regular Review Mechanisms**:
   - Implement a spaced repetition system for review, using flashcards or apps that schedule reviews at increasing intervals.
7. **Progress Monitoring Tools**:
   - Utilize apps or planners with built-in progress trackers that visually display your advancement through different topics and practice exams.

By tailoring these strategies to your learning style and schedule, you can create an efficient and structured study plan that can enhance your preparation for the BCBA exam.

***

Tips for Memorization and Conceptual Understanding

Here are some tips for memorization and conceptual understanding:

1. **Active Engagement**: Don't just read; engage with the material. Write summaries, create mind maps, or teach the concept to someone else.
2. **Mnemonics**: Use acronyms, rhymes, or associations to remember lists or sequences.
3. **Spaced Repetition**: Review the material at increasing intervals over time. This technique leverages the psychological spacing effect.
4. **Elaborative Rehearsal**: Connect new information to things you already know. Relate concepts to personal experiences or existing knowledge.

5. **Visualization**: Turn complex information into charts, graphs, or images.
6. **Application**: Apply concepts to practical scenarios or problems. Practice with diverse examples to deepen understanding.
7. **Self-Testing**: Regularly test yourself on the material to check your recall and understanding.
8. **Discussion and Collaboration**: Discuss concepts with peers or in study groups to gain different perspectives and insights.
9. **Rest and Nutrition**: Ensure adequate rest and good nutrition; brain function is closely tied to physical health.
10. **Mindfulness and Focus**: Use mindfulness techniques to improve focus during study sessions.

Implementing these strategies can enhance both the memorization of facts and the deep understanding of concepts, which are both critical for success in examinations like the BCBA.

***

Chapter Ten

Practice Questions and Answers

These questions are intended to simulate the type of content and thinking required for the BCBA exam.

1. **Ethics**: What is the most appropriate action for a BCBA if they discover a colleague is fabricating data?
    - A) Ignore it since it's not your direct responsibility.
    - B) Report the incident to the supervisor immediately.
    - C) Discuss the matter with the colleague and advise them to stop.
    - D) Contact the client involved and inform them directly.
    - **Answer**: B) Report the incident to the supervisor immediately.
2. **Concepts and Principles**: Which schedule of reinforcement is most resistant to extinction?
    - A) Fixed Ratio
    - B) Variable Ratio
    - C) Fixed Interval
    - D) Variable Interval

- **Answer**: B) Variable Ratio

3. **Assessment**: What is the primary purpose of conducting a functional behavior assessment (FBA)?
   - A) To determine the antecedents and consequences of behavior.
   - B) To diagnose the individual with a specific disorder.
   - C) To evaluate the cognitive skills of the individual.
   - D) To train parents on how to manage their child's behavior.
   - **Answer**: A) To determine the antecedents and consequences of behavior.
4. **Behavior Change Procedures**: What is an essential feature of a token economy system?
   - A) The use of response cost only
   - B) The exchange of tokens for backup reinforcers
   - C) Unlimited access to tokens
   - D) The use of one type of token for all behaviors
   - **Answer**: B) The exchange of tokens for backup reinforcers
5. **Intervention and Behavior Change Considerations**:

Which intervention is most appropriate for teaching a new verbal behavior to a non-verbal child?

1. A) Response cost
2. B) Time-out
3. C) Discrete trial training
4. D) Satiation
5. **Answer**: C) Discrete trial training

6. **Measurement**: What is the benefit of using inter-observer agreement (IOA) in data collection?
   - A) It helps determine the social validity of the intervention.
   - B) It eliminates the need for external validation of data.
   - C) It assesses the accuracy and reliability of the data recorded.
   - D) It increases the frequency of the target behavior.
   - **Answer**: C) It assesses the accuracy and reliability of the data recorded.
7. **Data Analysis**: In a line graph depicting behavioral data, what does a descending trend line indicate?
   - A) The behavior is increasing.
   - B) The behavior is unchanging.
   - C) The behavior is decreasing.
   - D) The behavior has variability.
   - **Answer**: C) The behavior is decreasing.
8. **Experimental Design**: Which experimental design involves removing an intervention to see if the behavior returns to baseline levels?
   - A) Alternating Treatments Design
   - B) Changing Criterion Design
   - C) Multiple Baseline Design
   - D) Reversal Design
   - **Answer**: D) Reversal Design
9. **Philosophical Underpinnings**: Which concept is foundational to the science of behavior analysis?

   - A) Cognitive dissonance
   - B) Determinism
   - C) Phenomenology
   - D) Dualism
   - **Answer**: B) Determinism

10. **Supervision**: When providing supervision to a BCaBA, what is an important consideration for the BCBA?

- A) The BCaBA should work independently without supervision.
- B) The BCBA should delegate all responsibilities to the BCaBA.
- C) The BCBA should provide ongoing supervision and training.
- D) The BCBA is not responsible for the actions of the BCaBA.
- **Answer**: C) The BCBA should provide ongoing supervision and training.

Here are 10 additional practice questions for the BCBA exam:

1. **Question (Behavioral Assessment)**: What is the PRIMARY purpose of conducting a preference assessment?
   - A) To identify potential reinforcers for a client.
   - B) To determine the function of a behavior.
   - C) To assess the client's skill level.
   - D) To evaluate the effectiveness of an intervention.
   - **Answer**: A) To identify potential reinforcers for a client.
2. **Question (Ethical Practice)**: If a BCBA encounters a dual relationship with a client, what is the BEST course of action?
   - A) Continue the relationship as long as it benefits the client.

- B) Terminate the relationship immediately.
- C) Seek supervision or consultation to navigate the relationship.
- D) Ignore the dual relationship as it is unavoidable.
- **Answer**: C) Seek supervision or consultation to navigate the relationship.

3. **Question (Experimental Design)**: What is the purpose of a reversal design in ABA research?
   - A) To compare two different interventions.
   - B) To demonstrate the effects of an intervention by removing it.
   - C) To establish a baseline for behavior.
   - D) To identify the function of a behavior.
   - **Answer**: B) To demonstrate the effects of an intervention by removing it.
4. **Question (Functional Behavior Assessment)**: A functional behavior assessment (FBA) typically includes which of the following components?
   - A) Direct observation and interviews.
   - B) Standardized testing only.
   - C) Medication review.
   - D) Intelligence testing.
   - **Answer**: A) Direct observation and interviews.
5. **Question (Philosophical Underpinnings)**: Which principle is MOST associated with the concept of 'selection by consequences'?
   - A) Generalization
   - B) Shaping
   - C) Extinction

- D) Operant conditioning
- **Answer**: D) Operant conditioning

6. **Question (Behavior Change Systems)**: What is an essential feature of a token economy?
   - A) Providing tokens that can be exchanged for a variety of backup reinforcers.
   - B) Using a response cost procedure.
   - C) Delivering continuous reinforcement.
   - D) Implementing a fixed ratio schedule of reinforcement.
   - **Answer**: A) Providing tokens that can be exchanged for a variety of backup reinforcers.
7. **Question (Measurement, Data Display, and Interpretation)**: What does a 'cumulative record' in behavior analysis show?
   - A) The total duration of a behavior over time.
   - B) The total count of a behavior over time.
   - C) The frequency of a behavior in different intervals.
   - D) The intensity of a behavior.
   - **Answer**: B) The total count of a behavior over time.
8. **Question (Behavior-Change Considerations)**: What is a potential drawback of using punishment in a behavior change program?
   - A) It can lead to quick reduction in behavior.
   - B) It may produce undesirable emotional responses.
   - C) It is the most effective way to reduce behavior.

  - D) It always requires reinforcement for effectiveness.
  - **Answer**: B) It may produce undesirable emotional responses.

9. **Question (Intervention and Behavior-Change Strategies)**: What is a primary goal of using a response interruption and redirection (RIRD) strategy?
    - A) To decrease the occurrence of repetitive or stereotypic behaviors.
    - B) To increase communication skills.
    - C) To reinforce alternative behaviors.
    - D) To provide sensory stimulation.
    - **Answer**: A) To decrease the occurrence of repetitive or stereotypic behaviors.
10. **Question (Supervision and Training)**: What is an important focus during the initial stages of a supervisory relationship in ABA?

- A) Discussing the supervisee's personal life.
- B) Establishing clear expectations and goals for supervision.
- C) Focusing solely on intervention techniques.
- D) Prioritizing administrative tasks over clinical ones.
- **Answer**: B) Establishing clear expectations and goals for supervision.

Here are 10 additional practice questions for the BCBA exam:

1. **Crisis Management**: What is the first step a BCBA should take when encountering a client in a severe behavioral crisis?
    - A) Implement a time-out procedure.
    - B) Ensure the safety of the client and others.
    - C) Immediately call for medical assistance.

- D) Begin a functional behavior assessment.
- **Answer**: B) Ensure the safety of the client and others.

2. **Behavior Reduction**: Which is an essential component when developing a behavior reduction plan?
   - A) Choosing the most restrictive intervention.
   - B) Identifying and defining the target behavior.
   - C) Implementing punishment procedures.
   - D) Focusing solely on consequences.
   - **Answer**: B) Identifying and defining the target behavior.
3. **Reinforcement Schedules**: What type of reinforcement schedule is used when a behavior is reinforced after a variable amount of time has passed?
   - A) Fixed Ratio (FR)
   - B) Variable Ratio (VR)
   - C) Fixed Interval (FI)
   - D) Variable Interval (VI)
   - **Answer**: D) Variable Interval (VI)
4. **Functional Communication Training**: What is the primary goal of Functional Communication Training (FCT)?
   - A) To teach alternative behaviors to replace maladaptive ones.
   - B) To use punishment to reduce undesired behaviors.
   - C) To increase the frequency of verbal speech.
   - D) To train caregivers in behavior management.
   - **Answer**: A) To teach alternative behaviors to replace maladaptive ones.

5. **Ethical Dilemmas**: If a BCBA finds that a recommended intervention conflicts with a family's cultural beliefs, what is the best course of action?
    - A) Discontinue services.
    - B) Modify the intervention to respect the family's culture.
    - C) Insist on implementing the intervention as planned.
    - D) Report the family for non-compliance.
    - **Answer**: B) Modify the intervention to respect the family's culture.
6. **Verbal Behavior**: According to Skinner's analysis of verbal behavior, what is an "echoic" response?
    - A) A vocal response that is identical to the verbal stimulus.
    - B) A response that is reinforced through social interaction.
    - C) A non-vocal mimicry of a model's behavior.
    - D) A vocal response to a non-verbal stimulus.
    - **Answer**: A) A vocal response that is identical to the verbal stimulus.
7. **Research Design**: In single-subject research, what is the main purpose of using a baseline phase?
    - A) To provide a comparison for the intervention phase.
    - B) To serve as the intervention itself.
    - C) To assess the subject's learning speed.
    - D) To train the subject for the intervention phase.
    - **Answer**: A) To provide a comparison for the intervention phase.
8. **Behavioral Skills Training (BST)**: What are the four components of Behavioral Skills Training (BST)?

- A) Prompting, fading, shaping, and reinforcement.
- B) Instruction, modeling, rehearsal, and feedback.
- C) Assessment, planning, intervention, and evaluation.
- D) Modeling, prompting, differential reinforcement, and fading.
- **Answer**: B) Instruction, modeling, rehearsal, and feedback.

9. **Generalization Strategies**: What is one effective strategy to promote generalization of a skill or behavior?
   - A) Training in one setting only.
   - B) Using a variety of stimuli and settings.
   - C) Limiting the number of trainers.
   - D) Focusing on discrete trial training only.
   - **Answer**: B) Using a variety of stimuli and settings.
10. **Parent Training and Involvement**: What is a key component when training parents in ABA techniques for their children?

- A) Ensuring parents strictly adhere to professional protocols.
- B) Teaching parents to conduct formal assessments.
- C) Encouraging parents to take over the therapist's role.
- D) Empowering parents with skills to effectively support their child's learning.
- **Answer**: D) Empowering parents with skills to effectively support their child's learning.

Here are 10 additional practice questions for the BCBA exam:

1. **Crisis Management**: What is the first step a BCBA should take when encoun-

tering a client in a severe behavioral crisis?

- A) Implement a time-out procedure.
- B) Ensure the safety of the client and others.
- C) Immediately call for medical assistance.
- D) Begin a functional behavior assessment.
- **Answer**: B) Ensure the safety of the client and others.

2. **Behavior Reduction**: Which is an essential component when developing a behavior reduction plan?
   - A) Choosing the most restrictive intervention.
   - B) Identifying and defining the target behavior.
   - C) Implementing punishment procedures.
   - D) Focusing solely on consequences.
   - **Answer**: B) Identifying and defining the target behavior.
3. **Reinforcement Schedules**: What type of reinforcement schedule is used when a behavior is reinforced after a variable amount of time has passed?
   - A) Fixed Ratio (FR)
   - B) Variable Ratio (VR)
   - C) Fixed Interval (FI)
   - D) Variable Interval (VI)
   - **Answer**: D) Variable Interval (VI)
4. **Functional Communication Training**: What is the primary goal of Functional Communication Training (FCT)?
   - A) To teach alternative behaviors to replace maladaptive ones.

- B) To use punishment to reduce undesired behaviors.
- C) To increase the frequency of verbal speech.
- D) To train caregivers in behavior management.
- **Answer**: A) To teach alternative behaviors to replace maladaptive ones.

5. **Ethical Dilemmas**: If a BCBA finds that a recommended intervention conflicts with a family's cultural beliefs, what is the best course of action?
   - A) Discontinue services.
   - B) Modify the intervention to respect the family's culture.
   - C) Insist on implementing the intervention as planned.
   - D) Report the family for non-compliance.
   - **Answer**: B) Modify the intervention to respect the family's culture.
6. **Verbal Behavior**: According to Skinner's analysis of verbal behavior, what is an "echoic" response?
   - A) A vocal response that is identical to the verbal stimulus.
   - B) A response that is reinforced through social interaction.
   - C) A non-vocal mimicry of a model's behavior.
   - D) A vocal response to a non-verbal stimulus.
   - **Answer**: A) A vocal response that is identical to the verbal stimulus.
7. **Research Design**: In single-subject research, what is the main purpose of using a baseline phase?
   - A) To provide a comparison for the intervention phase.
   - B) To serve as the intervention itself.
   - C) To assess the subject's learning speed.

- D) To train the subject for the intervention phase.
- **Answer**: A) To provide a comparison for the intervention phase.

8. **Behavioral Skills Training (BST)**: What are the four components of Behavioral Skills Training (BST)?
    - A) Prompting, fading, shaping, and reinforcement.
    - B) Instruction, modeling, rehearsal, and feedback.
    - C) Assessment, planning, intervention, and evaluation.
    - D) Modeling, prompting, differential reinforcement, and fading.
    - **Answer**: B) Instruction, modeling, rehearsal, and feedback.
9. **Generalization Strategies**: What is one effective strategy to promote generalization of a skill or behavior?
    - A) Training in one setting only.
    - B) Using a variety of stimuli and settings.
    - C) Limiting the number of trainers.
    - D) Focusing on discrete trial training only.
    - **Answer**: B) Using a variety of stimuli and settings.
10. **Parent Training and Involvement**: What is a key component when training parents in ABA techniques for their children?

- A) Ensuring parents strictly adhere to professional protocols.
- B) Teaching parents to conduct formal assessments.
- C) Encouraging parents to take over the therapist's role.
- D) Empowering parents with skills to effectively support their child's learning.
- **Answer**: D) Empowering parents with skills to effectively support their child's

learning.

Here are 10 more practice questions and answers for BCBA exam preparation:

1. **Behavioral Economics**: How does 'behavioral economics' influence decision-making in ABA interventions?
   - A) By analyzing cost-effectiveness of interventions.
   - B) By prioritizing the most expensive interventions.
   - C) By disregarding client preferences.
   - D) By focusing solely on short-term outcomes.
   - **Answer**: A) By analyzing cost-effectiveness of interventions.
2. **Professional Development**: What is an essential component of a BCBA's professional development?
   - A) Focusing only on areas of current expertise.
   - B) Regularly attending behavior analysis conferences.
   - C) Avoiding new research and sticking to known methods.
   - D) Never collaborating with other professionals.
   - **Answer**: B) Regularly attending behavior analysis conferences.
3. **Social Validity**: What is the importance of social validity in ABA interventions?
   - A) To ensure interventions are appealing to the therapist.
   - B) To make sure interventions align with societal norms.
   - C) To guarantee the fastest results.
   - D) To confirm interventions are practical and acceptable to clients.
   - **Answer**: D) To confirm interventions are practical and acceptable to clients.

4. **Discrimination Training**: What is the goal of discrimination training in ABA?
   - A) To punish incorrect responses.
   - B) To teach a client to differentiate between stimuli.
   - C) To focus on one stimulus only.
   - D) To provide reinforcement on a fixed schedule.
   - **Answer**: B) To teach a client to differentiate between stimuli.
5. **Stimulus Control Transfer**: What is involved in transferring stimulus control?
   - A) Changing the behavior being taught.
   - B) Shifting the control of a behavior from one stimulus to another.
   - C) Using the same stimulus in all settings.
   - D) Removing all stimuli associated with a behavior.
   - **Answer**: B) Shifting the control of a behavior from one stimulus to another.
6. **Task Analysis**: What is a primary use of task analysis in ABA?
   - A) To identify the most difficult task for the client.
   - B) To break down complex behaviors into smaller steps.
   - C) To determine the client's IQ.
   - D) To understand the therapist's tasks.
   - **Answer**: B) To break down complex behaviors into smaller steps.
7. **Motivating Operations**: How do motivating operations affect behavior?
   - A) They have no effect on behavior.
   - B) They alter the effectiveness of a reinforcer.

- C) They always decrease the frequency of behavior.
- D) They change the schedule of reinforcement.
- **Answer**: B) They alter the effectiveness of a reinforcer.

8. **Verbal Behavior Approach**: What is a key feature of the verbal behavior approach in ABA?
   - A) Ignoring the function of language.
   - B) Focusing on the form of language only.
   - C) Emphasizing the functional use of language.
   - D) Using language as the sole form of intervention.
   - **Answer**: C) Emphasizing the functional use of language.
9. **Pairing Process in ABA**: What is the purpose of the pairing process in ABA therapy?
   - A) To make the therapy environment aversive.
   - B) To establish the therapist as a reinforcer.
   - C) To pair all stimuli with negative outcomes.
   - D) To teach complex academic skills.
   - **Answer**: B) To establish the therapist as a reinforcer.
10. **Ethics in Research**: What is a critical ethical consideration when conducting ABA research?

- A) Only focusing on the outcomes regardless of methods.
- B) Ensuring participant consent and understanding of the research.
- C) Using any means to achieve desired results.
- D) Avoiding data collection and analysis.

- **Answer**: B) Ensuring participant consent and understanding of the research.

Here are 10 more practice questions and answers for BCBA exam preparation:

1. **Functional Behavior Assessment (FBA)**: What is the primary purpose of conducting an FBA?
   - A) To determine the punishment for a behavior
   - B) To identify the function of a behavior
   - C) To create a schedule of reinforcement
   - D) To train staff members
   - **Answer**: B) To identify the function of a behavior
2. **Positive Reinforcement**: What does positive reinforcement in ABA typically involve?
   - A) Presenting an aversive stimulus following a behavior
   - B) Removing a desirable stimulus following a behavior
   - C) Presenting a desirable stimulus following a behavior
   - D) Ignoring the behavior
   - **Answer**: C) Presenting a desirable stimulus following a behavior
3. **Extinction Procedures**: What is an extinction procedure in ABA?
   - A) Providing consistent reinforcement for a behavior
   - B) Increasing the frequency of a behavior
   - C) Withholding reinforcement for a previously reinforced behavior
   - D) Introducing a new behavior to replace an old one
   - **Answer**: C) Withholding reinforcement for a previously reinforced behavior

4. **Behavioral Contracts**: What is the purpose of a behavioral contract?

   - A) To legally bind a client to therapy
   - B) To outline specific behaviors and consequences agreed upon by parties
   - C) To document a client's progress for legal purposes
   - D) To serve as a formal punishment agreement
   - **Answer**: B) To outline specific behaviors and consequences agreed upon by parties

5. **Token Economies**: In ABA, what is a token economy primarily used for?

   - A) To provide immediate punishment for undesired behaviors
   - B) To reinforce desired behaviors through exchangeable tokens
   - C) To keep track of negative behaviors
   - D) To bribe clients into behaving appropriately
   - **Answer**: B) To reinforce desired behaviors through exchangeable tokens

6. **Ethics in ABA**: What is a critical ethical concern when practicing ABA?

   - A) Maximizing financial gain from therapy
   - B) Ensuring that interventions are based on the best available scientific evidence
   - C) Keeping therapy sessions as short as possible
   - D) Using only one approach for all clients
   - **Answer**: B) Ensuring that interventions are based on the best available scientific evidence

7. **Prompting and Fading**: In the context of ABA, what is the purpose of fading?

   - A) To gradually reduce the assistance provided to the client

- B) To completely remove a behavior from a client's repertoire
- C) To quickly introduce new and more complex behaviors
- D) To enhance the client's dependency on prompts
- **Answer**: A) To gradually reduce the assistance provided to the client

8. **Generalization**: What does generalization refer to in ABA?
   - A) Limiting behaviors to specific environments
   - B) The occurrence of a learned behavior in different environments
   - C) The decrease in frequency of a behavior over time
   - D) The process of teaching complex behaviors
   - **Answer**: B) The occurrence of a learned behavior in different environments
9. **Measurement in ABA**: Why is continuous measurement important in ABA?
   - A) To reduce the workload of therapists
   - B) To provide a comprehensive understanding of behavior patterns
   - C) To focus only on negative behaviors
   - D) To comply with insurance requirements only
   - **Answer**: B) To provide a comprehensive understanding of behavior patterns
10. **Cultural Competency in ABA**: What is the significance of cultural competency in ABA practice?
    - A) To adhere to standardized treatment protocols
    - B) To ensure that interventions are respectful and relevant to the client's cultural background
    - C) To avoid using any culturally specific interventions

- D) To prioritize the therapist's cultural beliefs
- **Answer**: B) To ensure that interventions are respectful and relevant to the client's cultural background

Here are 10 more practice questions and answers for BCBA exam preparation:

1. **Social Skills Training**: What is a key component when using role-playing in social skills training?
   - A) Focusing on punishment for social errors.
   - B) Using scripted scenarios to practice interactions.
   - C) Teaching clients to avoid social interactions.
   - D) Ignoring incorrect social responses.
   - **Answer**: B) Using scripted scenarios to practice interactions.
2. **Reinforcer Assessment**: How does a BCBA determine the effectiveness of a reinforcer?
   - A) By assuming all reinforcers work equally well for all clients.
   - B) Through trial and error during sessions.
   - C) By conducting a preference assessment.
   - D) Choosing reinforcers randomly.
   - **Answer**: C) By conducting a preference assessment.
3. **Ethics in Supervision**: What should a BCBA do if they suspect a supervisee of unethical behavior?
   - A) Ignore the behavior unless it becomes serious.
   - B) Confront the supervisee publicly.
   - C) Document the behavior and address it according to the ethical guide-

lines.

- D) Terminate the supervisee immediately without investigation.
- **Answer**: C) Document the behavior and address it according to the ethical guidelines.

4. **Parent Training**: What is an essential strategy when training parents in ABA techniques?
    - A) Encouraging parents to be passive observers.
    - B) Providing hands-on practice and feedback.
    - C) Limiting training to theoretical knowledge.
    - D) Discouraging questions from parents.
    - **Answer**: B) Providing hands-on practice and feedback.
5. **ABA in Schools**: How can ABA be effectively integrated into a classroom setting?
    - A) By using ABA techniques only for behavior reduction.
    - B) Implementing classroom-wide positive behavior supports.
    - C) Focusing solely on individual students.
    - D) Excluding teachers from the intervention process.
    - **Answer**: B) Implementing classroom-wide positive behavior supports.
6. **Data Collection**: Why is it important to use operational definitions in data collection?
    - A) To ensure that data is subjective.
    - B) To allow for flexibility in data interpretation.
    - C) To ensure reliability and clarity in measuring behavior.

- D) To make data collection more complicated.
- **Answer**: C) To ensure reliability and clarity in measuring behavior.

7. **Punishment Procedures**: What is a consideration when using punishment procedures in ABA?
    - A) They should be the first line of intervention.
    - B) They are more effective than reinforcement.
    - C) They must be used with caution and ethical considerations.
    - D) They should be used frequently to ensure effectiveness.
    - **Answer**: C) They must be used with caution and ethical considerations.
8. **Verbal Behavior**: In Skinner's analysis of verbal behavior, what is a "mand"?
    - A) A type of echoic behavior.
    - B) A response that is reinforced through social interaction.
    - C) A request or demand made by the speaker.
    - D) A form of non-verbal communication.
    - **Answer**: C) A request or demand made by the speaker.
9. **Teaching New Behaviors**: What is shaping in the context of ABA?
    - A) Removing a stimulus to reduce a behavior.
    - B) Reinforcing successive approximations towards a target behavior.
    - C) Implementing a new behavior without reinforcement.
    - D) Using punishment to decrease a behavior.
    - **Answer**: B) Reinforcing successive approximations towards a target behavior.

10. **Ethical Considerations for Assessment**: What is a key ethical consideration during the assessment process in ABA?
    - A) To use the assessment to diagnose medical conditions.
    - B) To ensure assessments are tailored and relevant to the client's needs.
    - C) To conduct assessments as quickly as possible.
    - D) To use only one type of assessment for all clients.
    - **Answer**: B) To ensure assessments are tailored and relevant to the client's needs.

Here are 10 more practice questions and answers for BCBA exam preparation:

1. **Professional Boundaries**: When should a BCBA decline a gift from a client or their family?
    - **Answer**: A BCBA should decline a gift that could potentially affect professional judgment or create a conflict of interest.
2. **Intervention Strategies**: What is a primary consideration when selecting an intervention for a client with self-injurious behavior?
    - **Answer**: The primary consideration should be the intervention's effectiveness and safety, based on empirical evidence and tailored to the client's needs.
3. **Behavioral Contrast**: What is "behavioral contrast" and how can it affect a behavior intervention plan?
    - **Answer**: Behavioral contrast occurs when a change in reinforcement conditions in one setting leads to an opposite change in behavior in another setting. It can affect intervention plans by causing unexpected increases or decreases in behaviors.
4. **Pairing in ABA**: What is the purpose of pairing in the context of ABA therapy?
    - **Answer**: Pairing involves establishing the therapist or teaching environment as reinforcing to create a positive and effective learning context.

5. **Motivation in ABA**: How does a BCBA assess and utilize client motivation in therapy?
    - **Answer**: Motivation is assessed through preference assessments and observing what naturally motivates the client, and then incorporating these motivators into the intervention.
6. **Cultural Sensitivity**: Why is cultural sensitivity important in ABA practice?
    - **Answer**: Cultural sensitivity ensures that interventions are respectful, effective, and relevant to the client's cultural background and family values.
7. **Reinforcement Schedules**: What differentiates a fixed interval schedule from a variable interval schedule?
    - **Answer**: In a fixed interval schedule, reinforcement is available after a set amount of time, whereas in a variable interval schedule, the time before reinforcement is available varies around an average.
8. **Behavioral Function**: How is understanding the function of a behavior critical in developing an intervention plan?
    - **Answer**: Understanding the function allows for the creation of interventions that address the specific reasons why a behavior is occurring, leading to more effective and ethical treatment.
9. **Generalization and Maintenance**: What strategies can a BCBA use to promote generalization and maintenance of learned behaviors?
    - **Answer**: Strategies include teaching skills in various settings, using different materials, and involving multiple people, as well as planning for maintenance from the beginning of the intervention.
10. **Ethical Dissemination**: What is the responsibility of a BCBA in disseminating behavior analytic knowledge to the public?
    - **Answer**: BCBAs are responsible for sharing accurate, evidence-based information and clarifying misconceptions about ABA to promote understanding and ethical application of behavior analysis.

Here are 10 more practice questions and answers for BCBA exam preparation:

1. **Functional Communication Training (FCT)**: What is the primary goal of Functional Communication Training in behavior analysis?
    - **Answer**: The primary goal of FCT is to teach individuals effective communication skills as alternatives to challenging behaviors.
2. **Token Economies**: In a token economy, what is critical to ensure its effectiveness?
    - **Answer**: The critical aspect is to ensure that tokens are consistently delivered for target behaviors and can be exchanged for meaningful reinforcers.
3. **Behavioral Skills Training (BST)**: What are the key components of Behavioral Skills Training?
    - **Answer**: The key components are instruction, modeling, rehearsal, and feedback.
4. **Measurement of Behavior**: Why is an interobserver agreement (IOA) important in behavior analysis?
    - **Answer**: IOA is crucial for ensuring the reliability and validity of data collected on behavior.
5. **Extinction Procedures**: What is an extinction burst and how should it be handled in a behavior intervention plan?
    - **Answer**: An extinction burst is an initial increase in the frequency or intensity of the behavior when extinction is first implemented. It should be anticipated and planned for in the intervention, ensuring consistency in not reinforcing the behavior.
6. **Task Analysis**: What is task analysis in ABA, and how is it applied?
    - **Answer**: Task analysis involves breaking down complex skills into smaller, teachable units and teaching each step systematically.

7. **Preference Assessments**: What types of preference assessments can a BCBA use, and in what contexts?
    - **Answer**: A BCBA can use various types, such as single-item, paired-choice, or multiple stimulus assessments, depending on the client's abilities and the context of the intervention.
8. **Ethical Reporting**: How should a BCBA handle discrepancies found in billing or service documentation?
    - **Answer**: Discrepancies should be promptly and ethically addressed, corrected, and reported to the appropriate parties, following legal and ethical guidelines.
9. **ABA and Autism**: How is ABA therapy tailored for clients with autism?
    - **Answer**: ABA therapy for clients with autism is individualized, focusing on social, communication, and behavioral skills, and often involves family training and collaboration with other professionals.
10. **Verbal Operants**: In Skinner's analysis of verbal behavior, what distinguishes a tact from an intraverbal?
    - **Answer**: A tact is a verbal response evoked by a non-verbal environmental stimulus (like naming what one sees), while an intraverbal is a response to verbal stimuli without the presence of the original stimulus (like answering a question).

With this comprehensive set of questions and answers covering a wide array of topics relevant to the BCBA test, you're equipping yourself with the essential tools needed for success. These questions not only enhance your understanding of key concepts in behavior analysis but also hone your critical thinking and application skills. They're designed to mirror the format and challenge of the actual BCBA examination, giving you a solid groundwork for what to expect. Keep pushing forward with your studies, and remember: You've got this! With dedication, perseverance, and these practice resources, you're well on your way to acing the BCBA test.

***

Tips for Analyzing and Answering Exam Questions

Tips for analyzing and answering exam questions, especially for a rigorous test like the BCBA exam, are invaluable for test-takers to maximize their performance. Here are some strategies:

1. **Read Carefully**: Make sure to read each question thoroughly. Pay attention to the details, as they often contain the clues needed to select the correct answer.

2. **Understand the Question**: Identify what the question is really asking. Is it looking for a definition, an application of a principle, or an analysis of a scenario? Knowing this will guide your thinking process.

3. **Key Terms**: Look out for key terms or phrases that are central to behavior analysis, such as "reinforcement," "punishment," or "functional assessment." These terms often indicate which concept the question is based on.

4. **Eliminate Wrong Answers**: If the question is multiple-choice, start by eliminating the options that are clearly incorrect. This increases your chances if you need to guess.

5. **Refer to the Literature**: Think about the relevant theories and studies from the behavior analysis literature that apply to the question. Sometimes recalling the source can help clarify concepts.

6. **Time Management**: Don't spend too much time on one question. If you're stuck, move on and come back to it later if time permits.

7. **Answer From a Behavior Analyst's Perspective**: Remember the principles and ethics of the field and answer from a professional behavior analyst's standpoint.

8. **Practice Questions**: Use practice questions to familiarize yourself with the format and wording of the exam questions. The more you practice, the better

you'll become at understanding what is being asked.

9. **Review Your Answers**: If time allows, review your answers, especially those you were uncertain about. Sometimes a second look can provide new insights.

10. **Stay Calm and Focused**: Test anxiety can interfere with performance. Practice relaxation techniques and maintain a positive mindset to help stay focused during the exam.

Incorporating these tips into your study routine and remembering them during the exam can help you analyze and answer questions more effectively. With dedication to understanding the material and strategic exam approaches, you'll be well-prepared for the BCBA test. Keep pushing forward; your determination and hard work will pay off. You've got this!

Chapter Eleven

Resources for Further Study

For those preparing for the BCBA exam, having a list of recommended texts and journals is vital for in-depth study and staying current with the latest research and developments in the field of behavior analysis. Here are some widely recommended resources:

1. **"Applied Behavior Analysis" by John O. Cooper, Timothy E. Heron, and William L. Heward**: This textbook is considered a seminal resource for understanding the fundamental principles and procedures of behavior analysis.

2. **"Verbal Behavior" by B.F. Skinner**: Skinner's work is foundational for those studying the application of behavior analysis to language and communication.

3. **"Behavior Analysis for Lasting Change" by G. Roy Mayer, Beth Sulzer-Azaroff, and Michele Wallace**: This book provides comprehensive coverage of behavior analysis principles and their application to real-world issues.

4. **Journal of Applied Behavior Analysis (JABA)**: As a leading journal in the field, JABA publishes research about the application of behavior analysis to solve problems of social importance.

5. **Behavior Analyst Certification Board (BACB)**: The BACB website offers a variety of resources, including task lists, ethics guidelines, and articles that are essential for BCBA candidates.

6. **Journal of the Experimental Analysis of Behavior (JEAB)**: This journal

focuses on research involving the experimental analysis of behavior and is useful for those interested in the theoretical and methodological foundations of the field.

7. **"The Behavior Analyst"**: This journal publishes articles on theoretical, experimental, and applied topics in behavior analysis.

8. **"Ethics for Behavior Analysts" by Jon S. Bailey and Mary R. Burch**: This book provides an in-depth discussion of the ethical codes and scenarios that behavior analysts may encounter.

Remember that a well-rounded preparation involves both reading foundational texts and keeping up with the latest research through journals and ongoing professional education opportunities. Always check for the most recent editions and publications to ensure the most up-to-date information.

***

Online Resources and Communities

For BCBA exam preparation, there are numerous online resources and communities that can offer support, study materials, and discussion forums. Here are some types of resources and communities you might find helpful:

1. **Official BACB Resources**: The Behavior Analyst Certification Board's website provides a host of materials, including the task list, ethics code, and newsletters that are crucial for exam prep.

2. **ABA Blogs and Websites**: Many websites run by BCBAs offer insights into study tips, career advice, and ABA techniques.

3. **Online Study Groups and Forums**: Joining study groups on platforms like Facebook or Reddit can provide community support, resource sharing, and advice from peers who are also studying for the exam.

4. **Webinars and Workshops**: Look for webinars and workshops offered by ABA

professionals that cover exam topics and answer participant questions.

5. **Flashcard Sites**: Websites like Quizlet may have user-generated flashcards for the BCBA exam, which can be a handy tool for memorizing terms and concepts.
6. **YouTube Channels**: Some channels are dedicated to ABA content, with videos explaining various concepts and strategies that may appear on the exam.
7. **ABA Software and Apps**: There are apps designed to help with specific areas of practice, such as data collection and graphing, which can be useful for understanding these processes more deeply.
8. **Online Courses**: There are comprehensive online courses and modules that offer structured learning paths towards BCBA exam prep, some of which may include interactive content and practice quizzes.

Remember, while these resources can be incredibly useful, it's important to ensure that any content or advice you follow is up-to-date and aligns with the BACB's current standards and guidelines. Always cross-reference information with official materials.

***

Continuing Education and Professional Development

Continuing education and professional development are essential for maintaining competence in the field of behavior analysis and for fulfilling the ongoing requirements for certification renewal by the Behavior Analyst Certification Board (BACB). Here's how you might approach these aspects:

1. **Continuing Education Units (CEUs)**: BCBAs are required to complete a certain number of CEUs within a recertification cycle. These can be earned through various activities, such as attending workshops, conferences, webinars, or completing online courses that are approved by the BACB.
2. **Professional Workshops and Conferences**: Attending workshops and conferences not only provides CEUs but also keeps professionals updated on the

latest research, methods, and ethical practices in the field. Many of these events are now available online, making them more accessible.

3. **Graduate Courses**: Taking additional graduate-level courses in behavior analysis or related fields can contribute to CEUs and deepen one's knowledge base.
4. **Peer Review and Publication**: Engaging in research and contributing to peer-reviewed journals can be a form of professional development and may also count towards CEUs.
5. **Online Learning Platforms**: Platforms like Coursera, Udemy, or the BACB's own learning portal offer courses that can help with professional development and may qualify for CEUs.
6. **Mentorship and Supervision**: Serving as a mentor or supervisor for those entering the field or working towards their BCBA can be a rewarding way to earn CEUs and give back to the community.
7. **Self-Study**: Reading relevant books, journals, and research papers is a valuable way to stay informed and can sometimes count toward CEU requirements.
8. **Specialized Training**: Engaging in specialized training programs for certain populations or techniques (e.g., verbal behavior, acceptance and commitment therapy) can advance a professional's skill set.
9. **Networking and Professional Organizations**: Joining organizations like the Association for Behavior Analysis International (ABAI) can provide opportunities for networking, professional growth, and access to exclusive resources and events.
10. **Ethics Training**: Since ethics is a critical component of ABA practice, completing ethics-related continuing education is mandatory for maintaining certification.

Remember that the requirements for CEUs, including the types and number of units, can change, so it's important to refer to the latest BACB recertification guidelines to ensure compliance. Additionally, it's beneficial to create a professional development plan that aligns with your career goals and interests in the field.

Chapter Twelve

Appendices

An application checklist for the BCBA exam typically includes a number of key steps and documents that applicants must complete and gather as part of the certification process. While I cannot access the specific contents of the file you uploaded, a general BCBA Exam Application Checklist might include:

1. **Confirm Educational Requirements**: You must have a graduate degree from an accredited university where you completed a verified course sequence or department-approved coursework in behavior analysis.

2. **Coursework Verification**: Cross-check your transcripts to ensure that you have completed the required amount of graduate-level coursework in specific content areas as per the BACB's coursework requirements.

3. **Document Supervised Fieldwork**: You need detailed documentation of your supervised fieldwork, including hours, dates, and supervisor sign-off, meeting the criteria outlined by the BACB.

4. **Complete the Application Form**: Fill in the BCBA exam application form thoroughly. This form collects your educational background, fieldwork experience, and other pertinent information.

5. **Prepare Fees**: The application process includes fees for both the application and the examination, which are published on the BACB's website.

6. **Identification for Exam Day**: Ensure you have a valid, government-issued photo ID to present on the day of your examination.

7. **Background Check**: If required, consent to and complete any background checks that are part of the certification process.

8. **Agree to Ethical Standards**: Acknowledge and agree to uphold the ethical standards set forth by the BACB, demonstrating your commitment to professional conduct.

9. **Request Examination Accommodations**: If you have a documented disability, follow the BACB guidelines to request the necessary accommodations well in advance of the exam date.

10. **Exam Preparation**: Engage in rigorous study, utilizing various resources such as textbooks, peer-reviewed journals, online practice exams, and any other materials that align with the BACB task list.

Each of these steps should be approached thoughtfully and thoroughly to ensure that your application reflects your qualifications and readiness to become a BCBA. Always refer to the most recent guidelines provided by the BACB to ensure that your application checklist is up to date.

***

Glossary of Terms:

1. **Antecedent**: A stimulus or event that precedes a behavior and may influence its occurrence.

2. **Behavior**: An individual's observable and measurable actions.

3. **Consequence**: The event that follows a behavior, which may affect the future frequency of the behavior.

4. **Discriminative Stimulus (SD)**: A stimulus in the presence of which a particular response will be reinforced.

5. **Extinction**: The process by which a previously reinforced behavior is weakened by withholding reinforcement.

6. **Functional Behavior Assessment (FBA)**: A systematic method of identifying the purpose or function that a particular behavior serves for an individual.

7. **Generalization**: The occurrence of relevant behavior under different, non-training conditions without the scheduling of the same events in those conditions.

8. **Interresponse Time (IRT)**: The amount of time that occurs between two consecutive instances of a response class.

9. **Negative Reinforcement**: The strengthening of behavior because it removes or diminishes a stimulus.

10. **Operant Conditioning**: A form of learning in which the future probability of a behavior is affected by its consequences.

11. **Positive Reinforcement**: The strengthening of behavior by presenting a desired stimulus after the behavior.

12. **Prompt**: A cue or action to assist the learner in performing a desired behavior.

13. **Reinforcer**: A stimulus change that increases the future frequency of behavior that immediately precedes it.

14. **Response Cost**: The removal of a positive reinforcer following a behavior to reduce the occurrence of that behavior.

15. **Shaping**: A process of reinforcing successive approximations to a desired behavior.

16. **Stimulus Control**: A situation in which the frequency, latency, duration, or amplitude of a behavior is altered by the presence or absence of an antecedent stimulus.

17. **Task Analysis**: The process of breaking a complex skill or series of behaviors into smaller, teachable units.

18. **Verbal Behavior**: Behavior that is reinforced through the mediation of another person's behavior.

19. **Variable Ratio Schedule (VR)**: A schedule of reinforcement where a response is reinforced after an unpredictable number of responses.

20. **Token Economy**: A system of contingent reinforcement based on the systematic reinforcement of target behavior. The reinforcers are symbols or "tokens" that can be exchanged for other reinforcers.

This glossary provides a framework of basic terms that are critical in the field of behavior analysis and for understanding the content of the BCBA exam. Mastery of these terms and their applications is crucial for individuals preparing for certification in behavior analysis.

***

Index of Key Concepts and Authors

- **Applied Behavior Analysis (ABA)**: A scientific approach to understanding behavior and how it is affected by the environment. **Authors**: B.F. Skinner, John O. Cooper, Timothy E. Heron, William L. Heward.

- **Behavioral Skills Training (BST)**: A training package that includes instruction, modeling, rehearsal, and feedback to teach new behaviors. **Authors**: Miltenberger.

- **Conditioned Reinforcement**: A process where stimuli gain their reinforcing power through association with primary reinforcers. **Authors**: B.F. Skinner.

- **Discriminative Stimulus (SD)**: A stimulus in the presence of which a response is reinforced. **Authors**: B.F. Skinner.

- **Echoic**: A verbal operant involving a response that is identical to the verbal stimulus. **Authors**: B.F. Skinner.

- **Functional Behavior Assessment (FBA)**: Identifying the purpose or function that a particular behavior serves. **Authors**: Iwata.

- **Generalization**: The transfer of a response learned to one stimulus to a similar stimulus. **Authors**: Stokes and Baer.

- **Negative Reinforcement**: Strengthening a behavior by removing or avoiding a negative outcome or aversive stimulus. **Authors**: B.F. Skinner.

- **Operant Conditioning**: The use of consequences to modify the occurrence and form of behavior. **Authors**: B.F. Skinner.

- **Positive Reinforcement**: The presentation of a stimulus following a behavior that increases the likelihood of that behavior occurring in the future. **Authors**: B.F. Skinner.

- **Verbal Behavior**: An analysis of behavior that is reinforced through the mediation of another person's behavior. **Authors**: B.F. Skinner.

Chapter Thirteen

Congratulations

Congratulations on making it through this comprehensive guide to prepare for the BCBA exam! You've invested time in understanding complex concepts, honed your analytical skills, and familiarized yourself with the ethical framework that will guide your professional practice. As you approach exam day, remember to:

- Review key terms and concepts regularly.
- Take practice exams to build confidence and improve time management.
- Stay updated on any changes to the BACB guidelines.
- Balance study with rest to keep your mind sharp.
- Believe in yourself and the hard work you've put in.

Good luck on your journey to becoming a Board Certified Behavior Analyst. Your dedication and effort have brought you this far, and they will carry you across the finish line. You're well-prepared, and you're going to do great!

www.ingramcontent.com/pod-product-compliance
Ingram Content Group UK Ltd.
Pitfield, Milton Keynes, MK11 3LW, UK
UKHW021922190726
13853UKWH00002B/786